To:

_____

From:

_____

Date:

_____

BIBLE
WISDOM
for Your Life

BIBLE
WISDOM
for Your Life

Women's Edition

BARBOUR
PUBLISHING

Written and compiled by Donna Maltese.

ISBN 978-1-61626-675-2

Published by Barbour Publishing, Inc., P.O. Box 719, Uhrichsville, Ohio 44683 www.barbourbooks.com

Our mission is to publish and distribute inspirational products offering exceptional value and biblical encouragement to the masses.

Printed in China.

CONTENTS

Introduction

When you have questions, God has answers!

God's Wisdom for Your Life: Women's Edition is a compilation of more than one thousand Bible verses, categorized under seventy key life topics. Drawing from various Bible translations for ease of reading, this book features subjects such as Blessings, Comfort, Confidence, Forgiveness, Friendship, Healing, Physical Appearance, Prayer, Stress, Temptation, and Worry.

Each category is accompanied by a contemporary "life application" introduction, while quotations, prayers, and brief devotional thoughts are also scattered throughout—making *God's Wisdom for Your Life: Women's Edition* your one-stop resource for encouragement, challenge, and hope.

■ ■ ■

I

Abiding

"Man may work from sun to sun, but woman's work is never done." If that old couplet is true, how does woman ever refuel? By abiding in Christ. Simply awaken to Jesus' presence, stay in tune with Him throughout the day, and expect great things from His hand. Walking side by side with the One who loves us empowers us to do all and love all, through sun and shadow.

"Abide in Me, and I in you. As the branch cannot bear fruit of itself, unless it abides in the vine, neither can you, unless you abide in Me. I am the vine, you are the branches. He who abides in Me, and I in him, bears much fruit; for without Me you can do nothing."

JOHN 15:4–5 NKJV

The branch of the vine does not worry, and toil, and rush here to seek for sunshine, and there to find rain. No; it rests in union and communion with the vine; and at the right time, and in the right way, is the right fruit found on it. Let us so abide in the Lord Jesus.

HUDSON TAYLOR

He who dwells in the shelter of the Most High will abide in the shadow of the Almighty.

PSALM 91:1 NASB

They that trust in the LORD shall be as mount Zion, which cannot be removed, but abideth for ever.

PSALM 125:1 KJV

You may trust in the Lord too little, but you can never trust Him too much.

ANONYMOUS

And I will pray the Father, and he shall give you another Comforter, that he may abide with you for ever.

JOHN 14:16 KJV

Abiding in God changes our relationship with our fellow humans. We cannot keep our heads in the clouds as we walk with Jesus on earth. We must deal day by day with others and through our actions show them the love we have received.

He that loveth his brother abideth in the light,
and there is none occasion of stumbling in him.
1 JOHN 2:10 KJV

Whosoever abideth in him sinneth not: whosoever sinneth hath
not seen him, neither known him.
1 JOHN 3:6 KJV

"As the Father loved Me, I also have loved you; abide in My love.
If you keep My commandments, you will abide in My love, just as
I have kept My Father's commandments and abide in His love."
JOHN 15:9–10 NKJV

"I have come as a light into the world, that whoever believes in
Me should not abide in darkness."
JOHN 12:46 NKJV

*Abiding is an active service of trust in God that demands
much of us but also provides us with untold blessings.*

"If you abide in Me, and My words abide in you, you will ask
what you desire, and it shall be done for you. By this My Father
is glorified, that you bear much fruit; so you will be My disciples."
JOHN 15:7–8 NKJV

He that saith he abideth in him ought himself also so to walk,
even as he walked.
1 JOHN 2:6 KJV

*To abide with Christ—to stay with Him and to learn from Him—
is to continually receive eyes to see, ears to hear, and a heart to obey.*
ANGELA MCGUFFEY

Now he who keeps His commandments abides in Him, and He in him. And by this we know that He abides in us, by the Spirit whom He has given us.
1 John 3:24 NKJV

Whosoever hateth his brother is a murderer: and ye know that no murderer hath eternal life abiding in him.
1 John 3:15 KJV

Whoever transgresses and does not abide in the doctrine of Christ does not have God. He who abides in the doctrine of Christ has both the Father and the Son.
2 John 1:9 NKJV

> *Keep your life so constant in its contact with God that His surprising power may break out on the right hand and on the left. Always be in a state of expectancy, and see that you leave room for God to come in as He likes.*
> Oswald Chambers

And now, little children, abide in him; that, when he shall appear, we may have confidence, and not be ashamed before him at his coming.
1 John 2:28 KJV

2

Anger

The adage "Hell hath no fury like a woman scorned" seems to give women a bad rap, yet it does contain a kernel of truth. Women hang on to anger and resentment longer than men. But God would have us neither get mad, nor hold grudges. So ladies, when tempted to rant and rave, take a deep breath, gather your thoughts, pray, and then—and only then—speak. Leave the rest up to God.

Stop being angry! Turn from your rage! Do not lose your
temper—it only leads to harm.
PSALM 37:8 NLT

The best remedy for a short temper is a long walk.
JACQUELINE SCHIFF

The LORD is compassionate and merciful,
slow to get angry and filled with unfailing love.
PSALM 103:8 NLT

Then the LORD said to Cain, "Why are you angry? Why is your
face downcast? If you do what is right, will you not be accepted?
But if you do not do what is right, sin is crouching at your door;
it desires to have you, but you must rule over it."
GENESIS 4:6–7 NIV

And "don't sin by letting anger control you." Don't let the sun go
down while you are still angry, for anger gives a foothold to the devil.
EPHESIANS 4:26–27 NLT

*Wise anger is like the fire from the flint; there is a great ado to bring it
out; and when it does come, it is out again immediately.*
MATTHEW HENRY

For wrath killeth the foolish man, and envy slayeth the silly one.
JOB 5:2 KJV

Better to dwell in the wilderness, than with a contentious
and angry woman.
PROVERBS 21:19 NKJV

A man would prefer to come home to an unmade bed and a happy woman than to a neatly made bed and an angry woman.
MARLENE DIETRICH

A soft answer turns away wrath, but a harsh word stirs up anger.
PROVERBS 15:1 NKJV

As surely as rain blows in from the north,
anger is caused by cruel words.
PROVERBS 25:23 CEV

It's smart to be patient, but it's stupid to lose your temper.
PROVERBS 14:29 CEV

*For every minute you remain angry,
you give up sixty seconds of peace of mind.*
RALPH WALDO EMERSON

"For as churning cream produces butter, and as twisting the nose produces blood, so stirring up anger produces strife."
PROVERBS 30:33 NIV

Don't make friends with anyone who has a bad temper.
PROVERBS 22:24 CEV

If we followed God's advice in this verse, how many of us would have friends? Yet how true it is that if we want good relationships with others, we need to treat them well.

An angry person stirs up conflict,
and a hot-tempered person commits many sins.
PROVERBS 29:22 NIV

Provoke not your children to anger, lest they be discouraged.
COLOSSIANS 3:21 KJV

The peculiarity of ill temper is that it is the vice of the virtuous.
It is often the one blot on an otherwise noble character.
HENRY DRUMMOND

"But I say, if you are even angry with someone, you are subject
to judgment! If you call someone an idiot, you are in danger of
being brought before the court. And if you curse someone,
you are in danger of the fires of hell."
MATTHEW 5:22 NLT

Wherefore, my beloved brethren, let every man be swift to hear,
slow to speak, slow to wrath: For the wrath of man worketh not
the righteousness of God.
JAMES 1:19–20 KJV

3

Blessings

Each day we have a choice in how we will look upon our lives and the world around us. We can focus on our troubles, which inevitably leads to a negative, downtrodden mind-set. Or we can focus on our good fortune, leading us to praise God and expect more from His hand. Which do you choose today? Make it blessings!

The Lord had said to Abram, "Leave your native country, your relatives, and your father's family, and go to the land that I will show you. I will make you into a great nation. I will bless you and make you famous, and you will be a blessing to others. I will bless those who bless you and curse those who treat you with contempt. All the families on earth will be blessed through you."
GENESIS 12:1–3 NLT

Blessings are on the head of the righteous, but violence covers the mouth of the wicked.
PROVERBS 10:6 NKJV

If our only blessings were possessions, in heaven we would be the poorest of souls. But because God made Himself our best blessing, we are rich both here and for eternity.

LORD, you alone are my inheritance, my cup of blessing. You guard all that is mine.
PSALM 16:5 NLT

Then Jesus turned to his disciples and said, "God blesses you who are poor, for the Kingdom of God is yours. God blesses you who are hungry now, for you will be satisfied. God blesses you who weep now, for in due time you will laugh. What blessings await you when people hate you and exclude you and mock you and curse you as evil because you follow the Son of Man. When that happens, be happy! Yes, leap for joy! For a great reward awaits you in heaven."
LUKE 6:20–23 NLT

From his abundance we have all received one gracious blessing after another. For the law was given through Moses, but God's unfailing love and faithfulness came through Jesus Christ.
JOHN 1:16–17 NLT

God's blessings are dispersed according to the riches of his grace,
not according to the depth of our faith.
MAX LUCADO

Through Christ Jesus, God has blessed the Gentiles with the same blessing he promised to Abraham, so that we who are believers might receive the promised Holy Spirit through faith.
GALATIANS 3:14 NLT

" 'The LORD bless you, and keep you; the LORD make His face shine on you, and be gracious to you; the LORD lift up His countenance on you, and give you peace.' "
NUMBERS 6:24–26 NASB

I will bless the LORD at all times; His praise shall continually be in my mouth. My soul will make its boast in the LORD; the humble will hear it and rejoice.
PSALM 34:1–3 NASB

Lord, like the Israelites who entered the Promised Land,
we are thankful we may choose to receive Your blessings,
no matter how many troubles come into our lives.

"Today I have given you the choice between life and death, between blessings and curses. Now I call on heaven and earth to witness the choice you make. Oh, that you would choose life, so that you and your descendants might live! You can make this choice by loving the LORD your God, obeying him, and committing yourself firmly to him. This is the key to your life. And if you love and obey the LORD, you will live long in the land the LORD swore to give your ancestors Abraham, Isaac, and Jacob."
DEUTERONOMY 30:19–20 NLT

LORD, you are mine! I promise to obey your words! With all my heart I want your blessings. Be merciful as you promised. I pondered the direction of my life, and I turned to follow your laws.
PSALM 119:57–59 NLT

> *To love God is the greatest of virtues;*
> *to be loved by God is the greatest of blessings.*
> ANONYMOUS

Those who live only to satisfy their own sinful nature will harvest decay and death from that sinful nature. But those who live to please the Spirit will harvest everlasting life from the Spirit. So let's not get tired of doing what is good. At just the right time we will reap a harvest of blessing if we don't give up. Therefore, whenever we have the opportunity, we should do good to everyone—especially to those in the family of faith.
GALATIANS 6:8–10 NLT

It came about that from the time he made him overseer in his house and over all that he owned, the LORD blessed the Egyptian's house on account of Joseph; thus the LORD's blessing was upon all that he owned, in the house and in the field.
GENESIS 39:5 NASB

> *We are to turn our back upon evil, and in every way possible,*
> *do good, help people, and bring blessings into their lives.*
> NORMAN VINCENT PEALE

The godly always give generous loans to others,
and their children are a blessing.
PSALM 37:26 NLT

"Bring all the tithes into the storehouse so there will be enough food in my Temple. If you do," says the LORD of Heaven's Armies, "I will open the windows of heaven for you. I will pour out a blessing so great you won't have enough room to take it in! Try it! Put me to the test!"
MALACHI 3:10 NLT

Do not repay evil with evil or insult with insult. On the contrary, repay evil with blessing, because to this you were called so that you may inherit a blessing. For, "Whoever would love life and see good days must keep their tongue from evil and their lips from deceitful speech."
1 PETER 3:9–10 NIV

Sing to the LORD, bless His name; proclaim good tidings of His salvation from day to day.
PSALM 96:2 NASB

Reflect upon your present blessings of which every man has many—not on your past misfortunes, of which all men have some.
CHARLES DICKENS

Her children rise up and call her blessed; her husband also, and he praises her: "Many daughters have done well, but you excel them all."
PROVERBS 31:28–29 NKJV

"But I say to you who hear, love your enemies, do good to those who hate you, bless those who curse you, pray for those who mistreat you."
LUKE 6:27–29 NASB

4

Challenges

Challenges face us within and without. They test our resolve, character, and faith. Will we listen to that negative voice in our heads, as well as the naysayers around us, and retreat? Or will we determinedly go forward into the unknown, knowing that, through the power of the Holy Spirit, God will help us step out of our comfort zone? Be amazing. Meet the challenge.

Anyone who meets a testing challenge head-on and manages to stick it out is mighty fortunate. For such persons loyally in love with God, the reward is life and more life.
JAMES 1:12 MSG

> *Challenge is a dragon with a gift in its mouth.*
> *Tame the dragon and the gift is yours.*
> NOELA EVANS

They were just trying to intimidate us, imagining that they could discourage us and stop the work. So I continued the work with even greater determination. . . . So on October 2 the wall was finished—just fifty-two days after we had begun. When our enemies and the surrounding nations heard about it, they were frightened and humiliated. They realized this work had been done with the help of our God.
NEHEMIAH 6:9, 15–16 NLT

> *We are continually faced with a series of great opportunities*
> *brilliantly disguised as insoluble problems.*
> JOHN W. GARDNER

"Now's your opportunity!" David's men whispered to him. "Today the LORD is telling you, 'I will certainly put your enemy into your power, to do with as you wish.' " So David crept forward and cut off a piece of the hem of Saul's robe.
1 SAMUEL 24:4 NLT

> *Whatever you can do or dream you can, begin it.*
> *Boldness has genius, power, and magic to it.*
> W. H. MURRAY

When Saul and his troops heard the Philistine's challenge,
they were terrified and lost all hope.
1 Samuel 17:11 msg

"Don't be ridiculous!" Saul replied. "There's no way you can
fight this Philistine and possibly win! You're only a boy, and he's
been a man of war since his youth." But David persisted. . . .
"The Lord who rescued me from the claws of the lion and the
bear will rescue me from this Philistine!"
1 Samuel 17:33–34, 37 nlt

> *Life's challenges are not supposed to paralyze you,*
> *they're supposed to help you discover who you are.*
> Bernice Johnson Reagon

Test yourselves and find out if you really are true to your faith.
If you pass the test, you will discover that Christ is living in you.
But if Christ isn't living in you, you have failed.
2 Corinthians 13:5 cev

So we may boldly say: "The Lord is my helper; I will not fear.
What can man do to me?"
Hebrews 13:6 nkjv

Make the most of every opportunity.
Colossians 4:5 msg

> *Help me move out to meet my challenges in faith—not fear—*
> *knowing that with You, Lord, I can do anything!*

Today the Lord will help me defeat you.
1 Samuel 17:46 cev

Saul had his own military clothes and armor put on David. . .
but he was not used to wearing those things. "I can't move with
all this stuff on," David said. "I'm just not used to it." David took
off the armor and picked up his shepherd's stick.
1 SAMUEL 17:38–40 CEV

I have always grown from my problems and challenges,
from the things that don't work out, that's when I've really learned.
CAROL BURNETT

For God did not give us a spirit of timidity (of cowardice,
of craven and cringing and fawning fear), but [He has given us
a spirit] of power and of love and of calm and well-balanced
mind and discipline and self-control.
2 TIMOTHY 1:7 AMP

Opportunities to find deeper powers within ourselves
come when life seems most challenging.
JOSEPH CAMPBELL

5

Change

Women go through a vast array of changes—
physically, relationally, emotionally. Then there
are changes through loss—death of loved ones,
unemployment, recessions, etc. And through
gain—new husbands, newborns, inheritances,
and so on. Through all this upheaval, there
is one thing that remains the same: God.
No matter what changes are thrust upon us
or are of our own making, God is with us
from our beginning to our final end. Thank
God for His never-changing presence!

When Pharaoh let the people go, God did not lead them on the road through the Philistine country, though that was shorter. For God said, "If they face war, they might change their minds and return to Egypt."
Exodus 13:17 niv

We all have big changes in our lives that are more or less a second chance.
Harrison Ford

"He who is the Glory of Israel does not lie or change his mind; for he is not a human being, that he should change his mind."
1 Samuel 15:29 niv

Continuity gives us roots; change gives us branches, letting us stretch and grow and reach new heights.
Pauline R. Kezer

"If we humans die, will we live again? That's my question. All through these difficult days I keep hoping, waiting for the final change—for resurrection!"
Job 14:14 msg

Lord, who may dwell in your sacred tent? Who may live on your holy mountain? . . . Those who fear the Lord; who keeps an oath even when it hurts, and does not change their mind.
Psalm 15:1, 4 niv

For when the priesthood is changed, of necessity there takes place a change of law also. . . . (for they indeed became priests without an oath, but He with an oath through the One who said to Him, "The Lord has sworn and will not change His mind, 'You are a priest forever' ").
Hebrews 7:12, 21 nasb

Can an African change skin? Can a leopard get rid of its spots?
So what are the odds on you doing good, you who are so
long-practiced in evil?
JEREMIAH 13:23 MSG

Therefore we will not fear, though the earth should change and
though the mountains slip into the heart of the sea.
PSALM 46:2 NASB

Every beginning is a consequence—every beginning ends some thing.
PAUL VALERY

My enemies refuse to change their ways; they do not fear God.
PSALM 55:19 NLT

God grant me the serenity to accept the people I cannot change,
the courage to change the one I can, and the wisdom to know it's me.
UNKNOWN

The LORD has sworn and will not change His mind.
PSALM 110:4 NASB

Fear the LORD and the king; do not associate with those
who are given to change.
PROVERBS 24:21 NASB

"I have spoken, I have purposed, and I will not change My mind,
nor will I turn from it."
JEREMIAH 4:28 NASB

"I am the LORD, and I do not change."
MALACHI 3:6 NLT

6

Children

The Lord tells us to have a firm hand and
a big heart when it comes to little ones. In
love, we are to teach them about Abba Father,
provide them with a good example, and pray
for them. And they have much to teach us.
Be attentive to the children around you. Take
time to see the world through their eyes.

"All your children will have God for their teacher—
what a mentor for your children!"
ISAIAH 54:13 MSG

> *Lord, give me the words and the willingness to tell children*
> *about You, Your love, and Your truth.*

"I will give them singleness of heart and action, so that they will
always fear me and that all will then go well for them and for their
children after them."
JEREMIAH 32:39 NIV

Do not aggravate your children, or they will become discouraged.
COLOSSIANS 3:21 NLT

He who spares his rod hates his son, but he who loves him
disciplines him promptly.
PROVERBS 13:24 NKJV

> *Hugs can do great amounts of good—especially for children.*
> DIANA, PRINCESS OF WALES

> *Most assuredly God will require an account of the children from the*
> *parents' hands, for they are His, and only lent to their care and keeping.*
> A. W. PINK

Children are a gift from the LORD; they are a reward from him.
PSALM 127:3 NLT

> *We know the excitement of getting a present—we love to unwrap it to*
> *see what is inside. So it is with our children; they are gifts we unwrap*
> *for years as we discover the unique characters God has made them.*
> CORNELIUS PLANTINGA JR.

But Jesus said, "Let the children come to me, and don't try to stop them! People who are like these children belong to God's kingdom."
MATTHEW 19:14 CEV

Cradling the little one in his arms, [Jesus] said, "Whoever embraces one of these children as I do embraces me, and far more than me—God who sent me."
MARK 9:37 MSG

Every child you encounter is a divine appointment.
WESS STAFFORD

If anyone does not provide for his relatives, and especially for members of his household, he has denied the faith and is worse than an unbeliever.
1 TIMOTHY 5:8 ESV

He commanded our ancestors to teach their children, so the next generation would know them, even the children yet to be born, and they in turn would tell their children.
PSALM 78:5–6 NIV

I call to remembrance the genuine faith that is in you, which dwelt first in your grandmother Lois and your mother Eunice, and I am persuaded is in you [Timothy] also.
2 TIMOTHY 1:5 NKJV

Teach your children right from wrong, and when they are grown they will still do right.
PROVERBS 22:6 CEV

7

Church

The term *church* can apply to a physical building as well as a body of believers. Either way, it is a place where Christians pray, praise, and petition together. With Christ and His love as the cornerstone, the church is a living organism, made to touch the lives of others in His name. Amazingly enough, women had a strong presence in the early church, and they outnumber the number of men who attend today. Keep it up, ladies!

God has put all things under the authority of Christ and has made him head over all things for the benefit of the church. And the church is his body; it is made full and complete by Christ, who fills all things everywhere with himself.

EPHESIANS 1:22–23 NLT

The Christian does not go to the temple to worship. The Christian takes the temple with him or her. Jesus lifts us beyond the building and pays the human body the highest compliment by making it His dwelling place, the place where He meets with us.

RAVI ZACHARIAS

Christ also loved the church and gave Himself for her, that He might sanctify and cleanse her with the washing of water by the word, that He might present her to Himself a glorious church, not having spot or wrinkle or any such thing, but that she should be holy and without blemish.

EPHESIANS 5:25–27 NKJV

The uniqueness of the Church is her message—the Gospel. The Church is the only institution entrusted by God with the message of repentance of sins and belief in Jesus Christ for forgiveness.

MARK DEVER AND PAUL ALEXANDER

Now these are the gifts Christ gave to the church: the apostles, the prophets, the evangelists, and the pastors and teachers. Their responsibility is to equip God's people to do his work and build up the church, the body of Christ.

EPHESIANS 4:11–12 NLT

So I will call you Peter, which means "a rock." On this rock I will build my church, and death itself will not have any power over it.

MATTHEW 16:18 CEV

We will speak the truth in love, growing in every way more and more like Christ, who is the head of his body, the church. He makes the whole body fit together perfectly. As each part does its own special work, it helps the other parts grow, so that the whole body is healthy and growing and full of love.

EPHESIANS 4:15–16 NLT

> *God's children should learn to rid the Church of problems,*
> *not to add problems to the Church.*
> WATCHMAN NEE

If the follower refuses to listen to them, report the matter to the church. Anyone who refuses to listen to the church must be treated like an unbeliever or a tax collector.

MATTHEW 18:17 CEV

Those who sin should be reprimanded in front of the whole church; this will serve as a strong warning to others.

1 TIMOTHY 5:20 NLT

> *A church should be a power-house, where sluggish spirits*
> *can get recharged and reanimated.*
> SAMUEL A. ELIOT

My friends, I beg you to watch out for anyone who causes trouble and divides the church by refusing to do what all of you were taught. Stay away from them!

ROMANS 16:17 CEV

But God composed the body, having given greater honor to that part which lacks it, that there should be no schism in the body, but that the members should have the same care for one another. And if one member suffers, all the members suffer with it; or if one member is honored, all the members rejoice with it. Now you are the body of Christ, and members individually.

1 CORINTHIANS 12:24–27 NKJV

The Holy Spirit makes a man a Christian, and if he is a Christian through the work of the Holy Spirit, that same Spirit draws him to other Christians in the church. An individual Christian is not Christian at all.

R. BROKHOFF

8

Comfort

When a child skins his knee, chances are he'll run to his mother first for comfort. When women need comfort, we run to God. He doesn't promise that we won't have trouble in this life, but He does promise that He'll be with us when we do. What a comfort, knowing God is our shelter in the storm.

"I will comfort you there like a mother comforting her child."
ISAIAH 66:13 CEV

Shout for joy, you heavens; rejoice, you earth; burst into song, you mountains! For the LORD comforts his people and will have compassion on his afflicted ones.
ISAIAH 49:13 NIV

Comfort is not the absence of problems;
comfort is the strength to face my problems.
KEN HUTCHERSON

Even though I walk through the darkest valley, I will fear no evil, for you are with me; your rod and your staff, they comfort me.
PSALM 23:4 NIV

You have allowed me to suffer much hardship, but you will restore me to life again and lift me up from the depths of the earth. You will restore me to even greater honor and comfort me once again.
PSALM 71:20–21 NLT

Give me a sign of your goodness, that my enemies may see it and be put to shame, for you, LORD, have helped me and comforted me.
PSALM 86:17 NIV

Remember the word to Your servant, in which You have made me hope. This is my comfort in my affliction, that Your word has revived me.
PSALM 119:49–50 NASB

God blesses those people who grieve. They will find comfort!
MATTHEW 5:4 CEV

God didn't promise days without pain, laughter without sorrow,
sun without rain, but He did promise strength for the day,
comfort for the tears, and light for the way.
ANONYMOUS

I find true comfort, LORD, because your laws
have stood the test of time.
PSALM 119:52 CEV

There is a difference between receiving comfort and being comfortable.
God's comfort comes to those who suffer for their faith,
not those who are lying on their laurels.

"But woe to you who are rich, for you have
already received your comfort."
LUKE 6:24 NIV

Christ encourages you, and his love comforts you.
God's Spirit unites you, and you are concerned for others.
PHILIPPIANS 2:1 CEV

Praise be to the God and Father of our Lord Jesus Christ, the
Father of compassion and the God of all comfort, who comforts
us in all our troubles, so that we can comfort those in any trouble
with the comfort we ourselves receive from God. For just as we
share abundantly in the sufferings of Christ, so also our comfort
abounds through Christ.
2 CORINTHIANS 1:3–5 NIV

I serve you, LORD. Comfort me with your love,
just as you have promised.
PSALM 119:76 CEV

When people sin, you should forgive and comfort them,
so they won't give up in despair.
2 Corinthians 2:7 cev

> The world hardly knows the meaning of comfort. But the Spirit of
> God offers the best there is to have. When we come to Him in pain
> and faith, He touches our hearts in tender ways that no human can.
> Not only does He offer a shoulder to cry on, He uses His people to
> strengthen and encourage hurting Christian hearts.

God our Father loves us. He is kind and has given us eternal
comfort and a wonderful hope.
2 Thessalonians 2:16 cev

9

Compassion

When we think no one cares, that no one
understands, when we have nowhere to turn,
when we are parched for a loving word,
a tender touch, a helping hand, there is only
one way to go—up. Look up, seek God's
face, plead your case. He will rain compassion
down upon you until you overflow with love
and strength, and become a woman who's
a fountain of compassion for others.

Then the Lord passed by in front of [Moses] and proclaimed, "The Lord, the Lord God, compassionate and gracious, slow to anger, and abounding in lovingkindness and truth; who keeps lovingkindness for thousands, who forgives iniquity, transgression and sin; yet He will by no means leave the guilty unpunished, visiting the iniquity of fathers on the children and on the grandchildren to the third and fourth generations."
Exodus 34:6–7 NASB

If you seek God, your God, you'll be able to find him if you're serious, looking for him with your whole heart and soul. When troubles come and all these awful things happen to you, in future days you will come back to God, your God, and listen obediently to what he says. God, your God, is above all a compassionate God. In the end he will not abandon you, he won't bring you to ruin, he won't forget the covenant with your ancestors which he swore to them.
Deuteronomy 4:29–31 MSG

Man may dismiss compassion from his heart, but God never will.
William Cowper

The Lord is compassionate and gracious, slow to anger and abounding in lovingkindness. He will not always strive with us, nor will He keep His anger forever.
Psalm 103:8–9 NASB

Just as a father has compassion on his children, so the Lord has compassion on those who fear Him.
Psalm 103:13 NASB

Jesus, Thou art all compassion,
Pure unbounded love Thou art;
Visit us with Thy salvation;
Enter every trembling heart.
CHARLES WESLEY

For He will deliver the needy when he cries, the poor also, and him who has no helper. He will spare the poor and needy, and will save the souls of the needy. He will redeem their life from oppression and violence; and precious shall be their blood in His sight.
PSALM 72:12–14 NKJV

Shout for joy, you heavens; rejoice, you earth; burst into song, you mountains! For the LORD comforts his people and will have compassion on his afflicted ones.
ISAIAH 49:13 NIV

Remember, O LORD, Your compassion and Your lovingkindnesses, for they have been from of old.
PSALM 25:6 NASB

Bless the LORD, O my soul, and all that is within me, bless His holy name. Bless the LORD, O my soul, and forget none of His benefits; who pardons all your iniquities, who heals all your diseases; who redeems your life from the pit, who crowns you with lovingkindness and compassion.
PSALM 103:1–4 NASB

You, O LORD, will not withhold Your compassion from me; Your lovingkindness and Your truth will continually preserve me.
PSALM 40:11 NASB

Have mercy on me, O God, according to your unfailing love;
according to your great compassion blot out my transgressions.
PSALM 51:1 NIV

May the flood of water not overflow me nor the deep swallow
me up, nor the pit shut its mouth on me. Answer me, O LORD,
for Your lovingkindness is good; according to the greatness of
Your compassion, turn to me,
PSALM 69:15–16 NASB

[Mankind's] heart was not steadfast toward Him, nor were they
faithful in His covenant. But He, being compassionate, forgave
their iniquity and did not destroy them; and often He restrained
His anger and did not arouse all His wrath. Thus He remembered
that they were but flesh, a wind that passes and does not return.
PSALM 78:37–39 NASB

He who conceals his transgressions will not prosper,
but he who confesses and forsakes them will find compassion.
PROVERBS 28:13 NASB

> *Compassion is a two way street.*
> FRANK CAPRA

Light shines in the darkness for the godly.
They are generous, compassionate, and righteous.
PSALM 112:4 NLT

So the LORD must wait for you to come to him so he can
show you his love and compassion. For the LORD is a faithful
God. Blessed are those who wait for his help.
ISAIAH 30:18 NLT

For no one is abandoned by the Lord forever. Though he brings grief, he also shows compassion because of the greatness of his unfailing love. For he does not enjoy hurting people or causing them sorrow.
LAMENTATIONS 3:31–33 NLT

If we want to touch hearts for Christ, the gentle, tender virtue of compassion could mean more than a thousand words of argument.

"You must be compassionate,
just as your Father is compassionate."
LUKE 6:36 NLT

*Christianity demands a level of caring
that transcends human inclinations.*
ERWIN W. LUTZER

Are your hearts tender and compassionate? Then make me truly happy by agreeing wholeheartedly with each other, loving one another, and working together with one mind and purpose.
PHILIPPIANS 2:1–2 NLT

*The measure of a country's greatness is its ability
to retain compassion in times of crisis.*
THURGOOD MARSHALL

If someone has enough money to live well and sees a brother or sister in need but shows no compassion—how can God's love be in that person?
1 JOHN 3:17 NLT

10

Confidence

It's not self-confidence that we really need, but
God-confidence—assurance that God will help
us fight our battles, give us courage to spread
His Word, fill us with strength to deliver a child,
write a book, teach a class, or put our love on
the line. Today and every day, seek the Lord.
He will fill your heart and mind with confidence,
and nothing will be able to stand in your way!

"With him is only the arm of flesh, but with us is the LORD our God to help us and to fight our battles." And the people gained confidence from what Hezekiah the king of Judah said.
2 CHRONICLES 32:8 NIV

When all our enemies heard of it, and all the nations surrounding us saw it, they lost their confidence; for they recognized that this work had been accomplished with the help of our God.
NEHEMIAH 6:16 NASB

> *If you hear a voice within you say "you cannot paint,"*
> *then by all means paint, and that voice will be silenced.*
> VINCENT VAN GOGH

Don't put your confidence in powerful people;
there is no help for you there.
PSALM 146:3 NLT

> *It's hard to fight an enemy who has outposts in your head.*
> SALLY KEMPTON

Putting confidence in an unreliable person in times of trouble is like chewing with a broken tooth or walking on a lame foot.
PROVERBS 25:19 NLT

Her husband has full confidence in her and lacks nothing of value. She brings him good, not harm, all the days of her life.
PROVERBS 31:11–12 NIV

> *Don't live down to expectations.*
> *Go out there and do something remarkable.*
> WENDY WASSERSTEIN

"Only in returning to me and resting in me will you be saved.
In quietness and confidence is your strength."
Isaiah 30:15 NLT

"But blessed are those who trust in the Lord and have made the
Lord their hope and confidence."
Jeremiah 17:7 NLT

They were all filled with the Holy Spirit and continued to speak
God's Word with fearless confidence.
Acts 4:31 MSG

Forget about self-confidence; it's useless.
Cultivate God-confidence.
1 Corinthians 10:12 MSG

And he did rescue us from mortal danger, and he will rescue
us again. We have placed our confidence in him,
and he will continue to rescue us.
2 Corinthians 1:10 NLT

*Aerodynamically the bumblebee shouldn't be able to fly,
but the bumblebee doesn't know that so it goes on flying anyway.*
Mary Kay Ash

Christ now gives us courage and confidence,
so that we can come to God by faith.
Ephesians 3:12 CEV

*The light of starry dreams can only be seen
once we escape the blinding cities of disbelief.*
Shawn Purvis

This truth gives them confidence that they have eternal life,
which God—who does not lie—promised them before
the world began.
TITUS 1:2 NLT

I am not a has-been. I am a will be.
LAUREN BACALL

So do not throw away your confidence; it will be richly rewarded.
HEBREWS 10:35 NIV

Faith is the confidence that what we hope for will actually
happen; it gives us assurance about things we cannot see.
HEBREWS 11:1 NLT

Without a humble but reasonable confidence in your
own powers, you cannot be successful or happy.
NORMAN VINCENT PEALE

This is the confidence we have in approaching God:
that if we ask anything according to his will, he hears us.
1 JOHN 5:14 NIV

11

Courage

Every day is a test of our courage. Do we
believe God is walking ahead of us, with us,
and behind us? Have we prayed for Him to
help us stand up to the myriad challenges
before us? Today's woman needs to be as bold
as or bolder than the one who touched Jesus'
cloak and was healed. Take courage, daughters.
Your risk of faith will make you well!

"Be strong. Take courage. Don't be intimidated. Don't give them a second thought because GOD, your God, is striding ahead of you. He's right there with you. He won't let you down; he won't leave you."
DEUTERONOMY 31:6 MSG

Wait for the LORD; be strong and let your heart take courage; yes, wait for the LORD.
PSALM 27:14 NASB

Courage is fear that has said its prayers.
DOROTHY BERNARD

Energize the limp hands, strengthen the rubbery knees.
Tell fearful souls, "Courage! Take heart! God is here, right here, on his way to put things right and redress all wrongs.
He's on his way! He'll save you!"
ISAIAH 35:3 MSG

"Then this humanlike figure touched me again and gave me strength. He said, 'Don't be afraid, friend. Peace. Everything is going to be all right. Take courage. Be strong.' Even as he spoke, courage surged up within me."
DANIEL 10:18 MSG

Don't listen to the voice of fear; listen to the voice of faith.

She was thinking to herself, "If I can just put a finger on his robe, I'll get well." Jesus turned—caught her at it. Then he reassured her: "Courage, daughter. You took a risk of faith, and now you're well." The woman was well from then on.
MATTHEW 9:21–22 MSG

When I asked for your help, you answered my prayer
and gave me courage.
PSALM 138:3 CEV

Courage is as often the outcome of despair as of hope; in the one case
we have nothing to lose, in the other everything to gain.
DIANE DE POITIERS

But Jesus immediately said to them: "Take courage! It is I.
Don't be afraid."
MATTHEW 14:27 NIV

Joseph of Arimathea, a prominent council member, who was
himself waiting for the kingdom of God, coming and taking
courage, went in to Pilate and asked for the body of Jesus.
MARK 15:43 NKJV

You can't test courage cautiously.
ANNE DILLARD

"These things I have spoken to you, so that in Me you may
have peace. In the world you have tribulation, but take courage;
I have overcome the world."
JOHN 16:33 NASB

When they saw the courage of Peter and John and realized that
they were unschooled, ordinary men, they were astonished and
they took note that these men had been with Jesus.
ACTS 4:13 NIV

A timid person is frightened before a danger,
a coward during the time, and a courageous person afterward.
JEAN PAUL RICHTER

12

Creativity

We were made in the image of the Master Craftsman. It is He who has instilled in us a desire to create. When we bake, cook, sculpt, sew, crochet, knit, paint, write, or sing to praise and glorify Him, He will say, "It's all good!" So, ladies, give in to that artful urging. Garner your talents, resources, and courage to create!

In the beginning God created the heaven and the earth. And the earth was without form, and void; and darkness was upon the face of the deep. And the Spirit of God moved upon the face of the waters. And God said, Let there be light: and there was light.
GENESIS 1:1–3 KJV

Creativity—like human life itself—begins in darkness.
JULIA CAMERON

God created man in His own image, in the image of God He created him; male and female He created them.
GENESIS 1:27 NASB

While we have the gift of life, it seems to me the only tragedy is to allow part of us to die—whether it is our spirit, our creativity, or our glorious uniqueness.
GILDA RADNER

God saw all that he had made, and it was very good.
GENESIS 1:31 NIV

"I've filled him with the Spirit of God, giving him skill and know-how and expertise in every kind of craft to create designs and work in gold, silver, and bronze; to cut and set gemstones; to carve wood—he's an all-around craftsman."
EXODUS 31:3–5 MSG

Lord, fill me with the spirit of creativity, giving me the ideas, energy, and imagination to make something pleasing to me, You, and others.

God's glory is on tour in the skies,
God-craft on exhibit across the horizon.
PSALM 19:1 MSG

Then Moses called Bezalel and Aholiab, and every gifted artisan in whose heart the Lord had put wisdom, everyone whose heart was stirred, to come and do the work.
Exodus 36:2 NKJV

"Be strong and courageous, and do the work. Do not be afraid or discouraged, for the Lord God, my God, is with you. He will not fail you or forsake you until all the work for the service of the temple of the Lord is finished."
1 Chronicles 28:20 NIV

Rule of art: Can't kills creativity!
Camille Paglia

Yet you, Lord, are our Father. We are the clay, you are the potter; we are all the work of your hand.
Isaiah 64:8 NIV

But the pot he was shaping from the clay was marred in his hands; so the potter formed it into another pot, shaping it as seemed best to him.
Jeremiah 18:4 NIV

Creativity is allowing yourself to make mistakes.
Art is knowing which ones to keep.
Scott Adams

Then Peter arose and went with them. When he had come, they brought him to the upper room. And all the widows stood by him weeping, showing the tunics and garments which Dorcas had made while she was with them.
Acts 9:39 NKJV

*We all have creativity in us and we all are multi-dimensional and we
are all interested in a lot of things and that women are fabulous.
We can handle a lot of things.*
SUZANNE SOMERS

Does not the potter have the right to make out of the same
lump of clay some pottery for special purposes
and some for common use?
ROMANS 9:21 NIV

*Imagination is the beginning of creation. You imagine what you desire,
you will what you imagine, and at last you create what you will.*
GEORGE BERNARD SHAW

13

Death

Our finite minds often focus on the fact that death is an end, when in actuality it is also a beginning. All who are born will one day die physically. But those who have Christ will continue to live on in spirit, in love never ending. Woman, let Christ be eternally yours, and you will be eternally His, now and forever.

You make known to me the path of life; you will fill me with joy in your presence, with eternal pleasures at your right hand.
PSALM 16:11 NIV

"Very truly I tell you, whoever hears my word and believes him who sent me has eternal life and will not be judged but has crossed over from death to life."
JOHN 5:24 NIV

Since you have been raised to new life with Christ, set your sights on the realities of heaven, where Christ sits in the place of honor at God's right hand. Think about the things of heaven, not the things of earth. For you died to this life, and your real life is hidden with Christ in God.
COLOSSIANS 3:1–3 NLT

Lord, thank You for raising me to a new and eternal life in You. Help me die to earthly pleasures and live for heavenly treasures. I desire to live a life worthy of Your love and favor— today, tomorrow, and forever.

For we know that if the earthly tent we live in is destroyed, we have a building from God, an eternal house in heaven, not built by human hands.
2 CORINTHIANS 5:1 NIV

The king was talking with Gehazi, servant to the Holy Man, saying, "Tell me some stories of the great things Elisha did." It so happened that as he was telling the king the story of the dead person brought back to life, the woman whose son was brought to life showed up.
2 KINGS 8:4–5 MSG

Let the redeemed of the LORD tell their story—
those he redeemed from the hand of the foe.
PSALM 107:2 NIV

A human life is a story told by God.
HANS CHRISTIAN ANDERSEN

An expert in the law stood up to test Jesus. "Teacher," he asked,
"what must I do to inherit eternal life?". . . . " 'Love the Lord your
God with all your heart and with all your soul and with all your
strength and with all your mind'; and, 'Love your neighbor as
yourself.' "
LUKE 10:25, 27 NIV

Death is a challenge. It tells us not to waste time. . . .
It tells us to tell each other right now that we love each other.
LEO F. BUSCAGLIA

Sin pays off with death. But God's gift is eternal life given by
Jesus Christ our Lord.
ROMANS 6:23 CEV

For I am convinced that neither death, nor life, nor angels, nor
principalities, nor things present, nor things to come, nor powers,
nor height, nor depth, nor any other created thing, will be able to
separate us from the love of God, which is in Christ Jesus our Lord.
ROMANS 8:38–39 NASB

Life is eternal, and love is immortal, and death is only a horizon;
and a horizon is nothing save the limit of our sight.
ROSSITER WORTHINGTON RAYMOND

14

Depression

Whether because of failure, loss of a loved one or job, or erratic hormones, at some point we may suffer some type of depression. But there's good news! Jesus is acquainted with our grief. In Him we can find rest and relief. So run, don't walk, to the nearest prayer place. Cast your cares on the Lord. He and His angels are just waiting to take care of you.

Elijah was afraid and ran for his life. . . . He came to a
broom bush, sat down under it and prayed that he might die.
"I have had enough, LORD," he said.
1 KINGS 19:3–4 NIV

He was despised and rejected by mankind, a man of suffering,
and familiar with pain.
ISAIAH 53:3 NIV

Depression is the inability to construct a future.
ROLLO MAY

"You will pray to him, and he will hear you. . . .You will succeed in
whatever you choose to do, and light will shine
on the road ahead of you."
JOB 22:27–28 NLT

Noble deeds and hot baths are the best cures for depression.
DODIE SMITH

He lifted me out of the pit of despair, out of the mud and the
mire. He set my feet on solid ground and steadied me
as I walked along.
PSALM 40:2 NLT

Why are you down in the dumps, dear soul? Why are you crying
the blues? Fix my eyes on God—soon I'll be praising again.
He puts a smile on my face.
PSALM 42:11 MSG

He has put his angels in charge of you to watch over you
wherever you go.
PSALM 91:11 NCV

In moments of discouragement, defeat, or even despair, there are always certain things to cling to. Little things usually: remembered laughter, the face of a sleeping child, a tree in the wind—in fact, any reminder of something deeply felt or dearly loved. No man is so poor as not to have many of these small candles. When they are lighted, darkness goes away—and a touch of wonder remains.
"THESE SMALL CANDLES,"
TOMBSTONE INSCRIPTION IN BRITAIN

"Come to me, all you who are weary and burdened,
and I will give you rest."
MATTHEW 11:28 NIV

He makes me to lie down in green pastures;
He leads me beside the still waters. He restores my soul.
PSALM 23:2–3 NKJV

He gives power to the weak, and to those who have no might
He increases strength.
ISAIAH 40:29 NKJV

I've treated my own depression for many years with exercise and meditation, and I've found that to be a tremendous help.
JUDY COLLINS

In peace I will both lie down and sleep, for You, Lord,
alone make me dwell in safety and confident trust.
PSALM 4:8 AMP

"Cease striving and know that I am God."
PSALM 46:10 NASB

15

Desires

God promises to fulfill our godly desires but warns us against selfish ones. What do you desire? Examine the source—is it from the spirit or the flesh? If the former, pursue it; if the latter, run for your life. Not sure? Take it to God. He'll steer you in the right direction. And remember, your first and greatest desire should be to seek God; His greatest desire is that you find and remain in Him.

"Sin is crouching at the door; and its desire is for you,
but you must master it."
GENESIS 4:7 NASB

I count him braver who overcomes his desires
than him who overcomes his enemies.
ARISTOTLE

Like water spilled on the ground, which cannot be recovered,
so we must die. But that is not what God desires; rather,
he devises ways so that a banished person does not remain
banished from him.
2 SAMUEL 14:14 NIV

"Acknowledge the God of your father, and serve him with
wholehearted devotion and with a willing mind, for the LORD
searches every heart and understands every desire and every
thought. If you seek him, he will be found by you; but if you
forsake him, he will reject you forever."
1 CHRONICLES 28:9 NIV

May He grant you according to your heart's desire,
and fulfill all your purpose.
PSALM 20:4 NKJV

Delight yourself also in the Lord, and He will give you the desires
and secret petitions of your heart.
PSALM 37:4 AMP

Some prices are just too high, no matter how much you
may want the prize. The one thing you can't trade
for your heart's desire is your heart.
LOIS MCMASTER BUJOLD

"My God, I want to do what you want.
Your teachings are in my heart."
PSALM 40:8 NCV

But more than anything else, put God's work first and do what he wants. Then the other things will be yours as well.
MATTHEW 6:33 CEV

Praise the LORD. . .who satisfies your desires with good things so that your youth is renewed like the eagle's.
PSALM 103:2, 5 NIV

What evil people dread most will happen to them,
but good people will get what they want most.
PROVERBS 10:24 CEV

> *Some people wanted champagne and caviar when*
> *they should have had beer and hot dogs.*
> DWIGHT D. EISENHOWER

"My word that goes out from my mouth: It will not return to me empty, but will accomplish what I desire and achieve the purpose for which I sent it."
ISAIAH 55:11 NIV

> *Desire, like the atom, is explosive with creative force.*
> PAUL VERNON BUSER

People who are ruled by their desires think only of themselves. Everyone who is ruled by the Holy Spirit thinks about spiritual things.
ROMANS 8:5 CEV

Let love be your highest goal! But you should also desire the special abilities the Spirit gives.

1 Corinthians 14:1 NLT

You can have anything you want if you want it desperately enough. You must want it with an inner exuberance that erupts through the skin and joins the energy that created the world.

Sheila Graham

With this in mind, we constantly pray for you, that our God may make you worthy of his calling, and that by his power he may bring to fruition your every desire for goodness and your every deed prompted by faith.

2 Thessalonians 1:11 NIV

Desire is the key to motivation, but it's determination and commitment to an unrelenting pursuit of your goal—a commitment to excellence— that will enable you to attain the success you seek.

Mario Andretti

But those who want to get rich fall into temptation and a snare and many foolish and harmful desires which plunge men into ruin and destruction.

1 Timothy 6:9 NASB

I used to desire many, many things, but now I have just one desire, and that's to get rid of all my other desires.

John Cleese

16

Diet

Living in a beauty-obsessed society, we
sometimes have difficulty deciding what, when,
or how much we should eat. Some women are
gluttons; others seem to be slowly starving
themselves. The key is determining what you
need to stay healthy. Ask the Lord for guidance
and whatever willpower you may need to take
care of that temple of God you're living in.
And make sure you include sizable portions
of God's Word in your dietary program.

Do not join those who drink too much wine or gorge
themselves on meat, for drunkards and gluttons become poor,
and drowsiness clothes them in rags.
PROVERBS 23:20–21 NIV

Gluttony is an emotional escape, a sign something is eating us.
PETER DE VRIES

Let your moderation be known unto all men. The Lord is at hand.
PHILIPPIANS 4:5 KJV

"Please test us for ten days on a diet of vegetables and water,"
Daniel said. . . . At the end of the ten days, Daniel and his three
friends looked healthier and better nourished than the young men
who had been eating the food assigned by the king.
DANIEL 1:12, 15 NLT

I've been on a diet for two weeks and all I've lost is fourteen days.
TOTIE FIELDS

They are the enemies of the cross of Christ: whose end is
destruction, whose god is their belly, and whose glory is in their
shame—who set their mind on earthly things. For our citizenship
is in heaven.
PHILIPPIANS 3:18–20 NKJV

More die in the United States of too much food than of too little.
JOHN KENNETH GALBRAITH

Everything God created is good. And if you give thanks,
you may eat anything. What God has said and your prayer
will make it fit to eat.
1 TIMOTHY 4:4–5 CEV

Do you not know that your bodies are temples of the Holy Spirit, who is in you, whom you have received from God? You are not your own; you were bought at a price. Therefore honor God with your bodies.
1 Corinthians 6:19–20 niv

> *I've been on a constant diet for the last two decades.*
> *I've lost a total of 789 pounds. By all accounts,*
> *I should be hanging from a charm bracelet.*
> Erma Bombeck

Therefore let no one sit in judgment on you in matters of food and drink.
Colossians 2:16 amp

Do not let all kinds of strange teachings lead you into the wrong way. Your hearts should be strengthened by God's grace, not by obeying rules about foods, which do not help those who obey them.
Hebrews 13:9 ncv

Man does not live by bread only, but man lives by every word that proceeds out of the mouth of the Lord.
Deuteronomy 8:3 amp

> *You can't lose weight by talking about it.*
> *You have to keep your mouth shut.*
> Unknown

Every animal on earth, every bird in the sky, every animal that crawls on the ground, and every fish in the sea will respect and fear you. I have given them to you.
Genesis 9:2 ncv

Jesus said, "Do you still not understand? Surely you know that nothing that enters someone from the outside can make that person unclean. It does not go into the mind, but into the stomach. Then it goes out of the body." (When Jesus said this, he meant that no longer was any food unclean for people to eat.)
MARK 7:18–19 NCV

Your words were found, and I ate them, and Your word was to me the joy and rejoicing of my heart; for I am called by Your name, O LORD God of hosts.
JEREMIAH 15:16 NKJV

"I am the living bread which came down from heaven. If anyone eats of this bread, he will live forever; and the bread that I shall give is My flesh, which I shall give for the life of the world."
JOHN 6:51 NKJV

When you go out to dinner with an influential person, mind your manners: Don't gobble your food, don't talk with your mouth full. And don't stuff yourself; bridle your appetite.
PROVERBS 23:1–3 MSG

Set a guard, O Lord, before my mouth; keep watch at the door of my lips. Incline my heart not to submit or consent to any evil thing or to be occupied in deeds of wickedness with men who work iniquity; and let me not eat of their dainties.
PSALM 141:3–4 AMP

Rich, fatty foods are like destiny: they, too, shape our ends.
UNKNOWN

17

Discouragement

Discouragement comes to us through
circumstances, events, and people. It can come
when we're already down or after a spiritual high.
The Bible is full of examples of godly people—
Hagar, Rachel, and Hannah among them—who
were lifted out of discouragement by God, a feat
He still performs today. Just pray, stand firm,
keep your eyes on God, and grab hold of hope.
God will lift you up and, woman, you will roar!

God, save me, because the water has risen to my neck.
I'm sinking down into the mud, and there is nothing to stand on.
I am in deep water, and the flood covers me.
PSALM 69:1–2 NCV

"Do not be afraid nor dismayed because of this great multitude,
for the battle is not yours, but God's. . . . You will not need to
fight in this battle. Position yourselves, stand still and see the
salvation of the LORD, who is with you."
2 CHRONICLES 20:15, 17 NKJV

*One ceases to recognize the significance of mountain peaks if they are
not viewed occasionally from the deepest valleys.*
DR. AL LORIN

"So be strong and courageous! Do not be afraid and do not panic
before them. For the LORD your God will personally go ahead of
you. He will neither fail you nor abandon you."
DEUTERONOMY 31:6 NLT

I focus on this one thing: Forgetting the past and looking forward
to what lies ahead, I press on to reach the end of the race and
receive the heavenly prize for which God, through Christ Jesus,
is calling us.
PHILIPPIANS 3:13–14 NLT

*Edison failed ten thousand times before he made the electric light.
Do not be discouraged if you fail a few times.*
NAPOLEON HILL

Then God remembered Rachel; he listened to her and
enabled her to conceive.
GENESIS 30:22 NIV

Why are you in despair, O my soul? And why have you become disturbed within me? Hope in God, for I shall again praise Him for the help of His presence.

PSALM 42:5–6 NASB

She, greatly distressed, prayed to the LORD and wept bitterly. . . . It came about in due time, after Hannah had conceived, that she gave birth to a son.

1 SAMUEL 1:10, 20 NASB

David was greatly distressed because the men were talking of stoning him; each one was bitter in spirit because of his sons and daughters. But David found strength in the LORD his God.

1 SAMUEL 30:6 NIV

What is important is to believe in something so strongly that you're never discouraged.

SALMA HAYEK

Do not be anxious about anything, but in every situation, by prayer and petition, with thanksgiving, present your requests to God. And the peace of God, which transcends all understanding, will guard your hearts and your minds in Christ Jesus.

PHILIPPIANS 4:6–7 NIV

We must not become tired of doing good. We will receive our harvest of eternal life at the right time if we do not give up.

GALATIANS 6:9 NCV

You can be discouraged by failure, or you can learn from it. So go ahead and make mistakes, make all you can. Because, remember that's where you'll find success—on the far side of failure.

THOMAS JOHN WATSON SR.

"But seek first his kingdom and his righteousness, and all these things will be given to you as well. Therefore do not worry about tomorrow, for tomorrow will worry about itself. Each day has enough trouble of its own."
MATTHEW 6:33–34 NIV

Casting the whole of your care [all your anxieties, all your worries, all your concerns, once and for all] on Him, for He cares for you affectionately and cares about you watchfully.
1 PETER 5:7 AMP

One of the things I learned the hard way was that it doesn't pay to get discouraged. Keeping busy and making optimism a way of life can restore your faith in yourself.
LUCILLE BALL

Lean on, trust in, and be confident in the Lord with all your heart and mind and do not rely on your own insight or understanding. In all your ways know, recognize, and acknowledge Him, and He will direct and make straight and plain your paths.
PROVERBS 3:5–6 AMP

"These things I have spoken to you, so that in Me you may have peace. In the world you have tribulation, but take courage; I have overcome the world."
JOHN 16:33 NASB

Although the world is full of suffering, it is also full of the overcoming of it.
HELEN KELLER

Lord, in You I regain strength. Lift me above the fray. Fill me to overflowing with hope. And I will praise You all the more!

18

Divorce

Divorce is a painful process and not part of God's original plan. But our God is a compassionate God. And although He says He hates divorce (which should be prevented when at all possible), He does not hate the one who is divorced. So for those who have split, take heart. God was with you in the past, He's with you now, and He's already in your future. He is your forever Husband. You will never go it alone.

The man said, "This is now bone of my bones and flesh of my flesh; she shall be called 'woman,' for she was taken out of man." That is why a man leaves his father and mother and is united to his wife, and they become one flesh.
GENESIS 2:23–24 NIV

As the church submits to Christ, so you wives should submit to your husbands in everything. For husbands, this means love your wives, just as Christ loved the church. He gave up his life for her.
EPHESIANS 5:24–25 NLT

Love is a feeling, marriage is a contract, and relationships are work.
LORI GORDON

For those who are married, I have a command that comes not from me, but from the Lord. A wife must not leave her husband. But if she does leave him, let her remain single or else be reconciled to him. And the husband must not leave his wife.
1 CORINTHIANS 7:10–11 NLT

Work at getting along with each other and with God. Otherwise you'll never get so much as a glimpse of God. Make sure no one gets left out of God's generosity. Keep a sharp eye out for weeds of bitter discontent. A thistle or two gone to seed can ruin a whole garden in no time.
HEBREWS 12:15 MSG

Lord, uproot the bitterness that's taken hold of my heart. Help me to look to You, my ultimate protector, as my Husband, through thick and thin. Humans are fallible, but You are not. Thank You for coming to my rescue, for always being with me, and for Your constant mercy.

The Lord, the God of Israel, says: I hate divorce and marital separation and him who covers his garment [his wife] with violence. Therefore keep a watch upon your spirit [that it may be controlled by My Spirit], that you deal not treacherously and faithlessly [with your marriage mate].

MALACHI 2:16 AMP

The worst reconciliation is better than the best divorce.
MIGUEL DE CERVANTES SAAVEDRA

"You have heard the law that says, 'A man can divorce his wife by merely giving her a written notice of divorce.' But I say that a man who divorces his wife, unless she has been unfaithful, causes her to commit adultery. And anyone who marries a divorced woman also commits adultery."

MATTHEW 5:31–32 NLT

Being divorced is like being hit by a Mack truck. If you live through it, you start looking very carefully to the right and to the left.
JEAN KERR

"If anyone fiercely assails you it will not be from Me. Whoever assails you will fall because of you. . . . No weapon that is formed against you will prosper; and every tongue that accuses you in judgment you will condemn. This is the heritage of the servants of the LORD, and their vindication is from Me," declares the LORD.

ISAIAH 54:15, 17 NASB

"Return, faithless people," declares the LORD, "for I am your husband. I will choose you—one from a town and two from a clan—and bring you to Zion."

JEREMIAH 3:14 NIV

"For your Maker is your bridegroom, his name, God-of-the-Angel-Armies! Your Redeemer is The Holy of Israel, known as God of the whole earth. You were like an abandoned wife, devastated with grief, and God welcomed you back, like a woman married young and then left," says your God.

Isaiah 54:5–6 msg

"I will be true to you as my promised bride,
and you will know the Lord."

Hosea 2:20 ncv

And I saw the holy city, the new Jerusalem, coming down out of heaven from God. It was prepared like a bride dressed for her husband. And I heard a loud voice from the throne, saying, "Now God's presence is with people, and he will live with them, and they will be his people. God himself will be with them and will be their God. He will wipe away every tear from their eyes, and there will be no more death, sadness, crying, or pain, because all the old ways are gone."

Revelation 21:2–4 ncv

Even though you may want to move forward in your life, you may have one foot on the brakes. In order to be free, we must learn how to let go. Release the hurt. Release the fear. Refuse to entertain your old pain. The energy it takes to hang onto the past is holding you back from a new life. What is it you would let go of today?
Mary Manin Morrissey

19

Doubt

The Bible says we are strangers in this world,
sojourners upon the earth. Would that we all had
the faith of Abraham, an alien on this planet,
who, although he did not know where he was
going, trusted God to take him there. Ladies,
banishing doubt is a minute-by-minute process.
But we must endeavor to do so. For it is when
our faith is greatest that the greatest happens!

"Truly I tell you, if anyone says to this mountain, 'Go, throw yourself into the sea,' and does not doubt in their heart but believes that what they say will happen, it will be done for them."
MARK 11:23 NIV

If any of you lacks wisdom, you should ask God, who gives generously to all without finding fault, and it will be given to you. But when you ask, you must believe and not doubt, because the one who doubts is like a wave of the sea, blown and tossed by the wind. That person should not expect to receive anything from the Lord. Such a person is double-minded and unstable in all they do.
JAMES 1:5–8 NIV

And you must show mercy to those whose faith is wavering.
JUDE 1:22 NLT

But Abraham never doubted or questioned God's promise. His faith made him strong, and he gave all the credit to God.
ROMANS 4:20 CEV

My friends, watch out! Don't let evil thoughts or doubts make any of you turn from the living God.
HEBREWS 3:12 CEV

Worry affects the circulation, the heart, the glands, the whole nervous system. I have never known a man who died from overwork, but many who died from doubt.
CHARLES H. MAYO

I will therefore that men pray every where, lifting up holy hands, without wrath and doubting.
1 TIMOTHY 2:8 KJV

Yea, though I walk through the valley of the shadow of death, I will fear no evil: for thou art with me; thy rod and thy staff they comfort me.
PSALM 23:4 KJV

Light up. . .the lamp of faith in your heart. . . . It will lead you safely through the mists of doubt and the black darkness of despair; along the narrow, thorny ways of sickness and sorrow, and over the treacherous places of temptation and uncertainty.
JAMES ALLEN

When doubts filled my mind, your comfort gave me renewed hope and cheer.
PSALM 94:19 NLT

But if you have doubts about whether or not you should eat something, you are sinning if you go ahead and do it. For you are not following your convictions. If you do anything you believe is not right, you are sinning.
ROMANS 14:23 NLT

20

Ecology

After God created the earth, He instructed humans to tend and care for it. In our lifetimes, each of us is the current custodian for our section of the world. And right now, mother earth needs lots of help. So, ladies, roll up your sleeves. Let's get some earth keeping done as part of our daily worship! May the spiritual mark you leave upon this earth be a million times larger than your carbon footprint!

In the beginning God created the heavens and the earth. . . .
God saw all that he had made, and it was very good.
GENESIS 1:1, 31 NIV

Christ is the visible image of the invisible God. He existed
before anything was created and is supreme over all creation,
for through him God created everything in the heavenly realms
and on earth. He made the things we can see and the things
we can't see.
COLOSSIANS 1:15–16 NLT

Then the LORD God took the man and put him into the garden
of Eden to cultivate it and keep it.
GENESIS 2:15 NASB

> *There are no passengers on Spaceship Earth. We are all crew.*
> MARSHALL MCLUHAN

Then God blessed them and said, "Be fruitful and multiply. Fill the
earth and govern it. Reign over the fish in the sea, the birds in
the sky, and all the animals that scurry along the ground."
GENESIS 1:28 NLT

"If My people who are called by My name will humble
themselves, and pray and seek My face, and turn from their
wicked ways, then I will hear from heaven, and will forgive their
sin and heal their land."
2 CHRONICLES 7:14 NKJV

> *When we heal the earth, we heal ourselves.*
> DAVID ORR

"And if you defile the land, it will vomit you out as it vomited out
the nations that were before you."
LEVITICUS 18:28 NIV

The earth we abuse and the living things we kill will,
in the end, take their revenge; for in exploiting their presence
we are diminishing our future.
MARYA MANNES

The LORD will comfort Israel again and have pity on her ruins.
Her desert will blossom like Eden, her barren wilderness like the
garden of the LORD. Joy and gladness will be found there. Songs
of thanksgiving will fill the air.
ISAIAH 51:3 NLT

"Are not five sparrows sold for two cents? Yet not one of them is
forgotten before God."
LUKE 12:6 NASB

Lord, this earth is Yours—not ours. Give me the wisdom
to treat this wonderful world with loving-kindness.

Seemeth it a small thing unto you to have eaten up the good
pasture, but ye must tread down with your feet the residue of
your pastures? and to have drunk of the deep waters,
but ye must foul the residue with your feet?
EZEKIEL 34:18 KJV

When you defile the pleasant streams
And the wild bird's abiding place,
You massacre a million dreams
And cast your spittle in God's face.
JOHN DRINKWATER

"They have turned my field into a desert that is wilted and dead. The whole country is an empty desert, because no one who lives there cares."
JEREMIAH 12:11 NCV

When one tugs at a single thing in nature, he finds it attached to the rest of the world.
JOHN MUIR

For ever since the creation of the world His invisible nature and attributes, that is, His eternal power and divinity, have been made intelligible and clearly discernible in and through the things that have been made (His handiworks).
ROMANS 1:20 AMP

"You will go out in joy and be led forth in peace; the mountains and hills will burst into song before you, and all the trees of the field will clap their hands."
ISAIAH 55:12 NIV

"But ask the animals, and they will teach you, or ask the birds of the air, and they will tell you. Speak to the earth, and it will teach you, or let the fish of the sea tell you. Every one of these knows that the hand of the Lord has done this. The life of every creature and the breath of all people are in God's hand."
JOB 12:7–10 NCV

Every creature is better alive than dead, men and moose and pine trees, and he who understands it aright will rather preserve its life than destroy it.
HENRY DAVID THOREAU

21

Eternal Life

When you accepted Christ, your life became
unlimited—eternal! How great is that? Now and
forever you will be surrounded by God's love.
All you have to do is reach out for it. Nurture
that love, then spread it around, touching
everyone you come into contact with. Send God
a thank-you note for the gift of forever and
the life of today. Sign it, "Eternally yours."

"Anyone who believes in God's Son has eternal life. Anyone who doesn't obey the Son will never experience eternal life but remains under God's angry judgment."
JOHN 3:36 NLT

Eternity to the godly is a day that has no sunset;
eternity to the wicked is a night that has no sunrise.
THOMAS WATSON

"Very truly I tell you, whoever hears my word and believes him who sent me has eternal life and will not be judged but has crossed over from death to life."
JOHN 5:24 NIV

"My sheep hear My voice, and I know them, and they follow Me. And I give them eternal life, and they shall never perish; neither shall anyone snatch them out of My hand. My Father, who has given them to Me, is greater than all; and no one is able to snatch them out of My Father's hand."
JOHN 10:27–29 NKJV

Someone came to Jesus with this question: "Teacher, what good deed must I do to have eternal life?" "Why ask me about what is good?" Jesus replied. "There is only One who is good. But to answer your question—if you want to receive eternal life, keep the commandments."
MATTHEW 19:16–17 NLT

"Everyone who has left houses or brothers or sisters or father or mother or wife or children or lands, for My name's sake, shall receive a hundredfold, and inherit eternal life."
MATTHEW 19:29 NKJV

"What sorrow awaits the world, because it tempts people to sin. Temptations are inevitable, but what sorrow awaits the person who does the tempting. So if your hand or foot causes you to sin, cut it off and throw it away. It's better to enter eternal life with only one hand or one foot than to be thrown into eternal fire with both of your hands and feet. And if your eye causes you to sin, gouge it out and throw it away. It's better to enter eternal life with only one eye than to have two eyes and be thrown into the fire of hell."

MATTHEW 18:7–9 NLT

Nothing can separate you from God's love, absolutely nothing. God is enough for time, God is enough for eternity. God is enough!

HANNAH WHITALL SMITH

"For God loved the world so much that he gave his one and only Son, so that everyone who believes in him will not perish but have eternal life."

JOHN 3:16 NLT

The best we can hope for in this life is a knothole peek at the shining realities ahead. Yet a glimpse is enough. It's enough to convince our hearts that whatever sufferings and sorrows currently assail us aren't worthy of comparison to that which waits over the horizon.

JONI EARECKSON TADA

God will reward each of us for what we have done. He will give eternal life to everyone who has patiently done what is good in the hope of receiving glory, honor, and life that lasts forever. But he will show how angry and furious he can be with every selfish person who rejects the truth and wants to do evil.

ROMANS 2:6–8 CEV

So just as sin ruled over all people and brought them to death, now God's wonderful grace rules instead, giving us right standing with God and resulting in eternal life through Jesus Christ our Lord.

ROMANS 5:21 NLT

For the wages of sin is death, but the gift of God is eternal life in Christ Jesus our Lord.

ROMANS 6:23 NKJV

Lord, Your Word has given me a vision of eternity,
and the Spirit speaks of its certainty in my heart.
Let those who doubt never turn me from it.

For you have been born again, but not to a life that will quickly end. Your new life will last forever because it comes from the eternal, living word of God.

1 PETER 1:23 NLT

We know that we have passed from death unto life, because we love the brethren. He that loveth not his brother abideth in death. Whosoever hateth his brother is a murderer: and ye know that no murderer hath eternal life abiding in him.

1 JOHN 3:14–15 KJV

God showed how much he loved us by sending his one and only Son into the world so that we might have eternal life through him.

1 JOHN 4:9 NLT

22

Evil

Evil surrounds us—within and without. From the
tempting voice inside our heads to the criminal
on the street, we have only one defense: God and
His Word. So armor up, girls! Grab that shield
of faith. Take the sword of the Spirit out of its
scabbard. It's battle time, lionesses. Pray for a
hedge of protection between you and yours and
the evil one. Remember, God's on your side! And
you're a force to be reckoned with. *En garde!*

The Lord is watching everywhere,
keeping his eye on both the evil and the good.
Proverbs 15:3 NLT

God judged it better to bring good out of evil
than to suffer no evil to exist.
Saint Augustine

The serpent said to the woman, "You surely will not die! For God
knows that in the day you eat from it your eyes will be opened,
and you will be like God, knowing good and evil." When the
woman saw that the tree was good for food, and that it was a
delight to the eyes, and that the tree was desirable to make one
wise, she took from its fruit and ate; and she gave also to her
husband with her, and he ate.
Genesis 3:4–6 NASB

You are not a God who delights in wickedness;
evil may not dwell with you.
Psalm 5:4 ESV

We can be thankful that God does not remove all evil right now. If He
did, would He not remove you? Suppose He said, "Ok, I will do just
as you request. I will take away all evil right this minute!"
Do you think that you would be spared?
Jim Elliff

And I know that nothing good lives in me, that is, in my sinful
nature. I want to do what is right, but I can't. I want to do what
is good, but I don't. I don't want to do what is wrong, but I do it
anyway. But if I do what I don't want to do, I am not really the
one doing wrong; it is sin living in me that does it.
Romans 7:18–20 NLT

"That which proceeds out of the man, that is what defiles the man. For from within, out of the heart of men, proceed the evil thoughts, fornications, thefts, murders, adulteries, deeds of coveting and wickedness, as well as deceit, sensuality, envy, slander, pride and foolishness."
MARK 7:20–22 NASB

For our struggle is not against flesh and blood, but against the rulers, against the powers, against the world forces of this darkness, against the spiritual forces of wickedness in the heavenly places. Therefore, take up the full armor of God, so that you will be able to resist in the evil day, and having done everything, to stand firm.
EPHESIANS 6:12–13 NASB

The more praying there is in the world, the better the world will be; the mightier the forces against evil everywhere.
E. M. BOUNDS

"This is the verdict: Light has come into the world, but people loved darkness instead of light because their deeds were evil. Everyone who does evil hates the light, and will not come into the light for fear that their deeds will be exposed. But whoever lives by the truth comes into the light, so that it may be seen plainly that what they have done has been done in the sight of God."
JOHN 3:19–21 NIV

Turn your back on evil, work for the good and don't quit. God loves this kind of thing, never turns away from his friends.
PSALM 37:27 MSG

If Christ has died for me. . .I cannot trifle with the evil that slew my
best friend. I must be holy for His sake. How can I live in sin when
He has died to save me from it?
C. H. SPURGEON

Keep your tongue from evil and your lips from speaking deceit.
Depart from evil and do good; seek peace and pursue it.
PSALM 34:13–14 NASB

Do not fret because of those who are evil or be envious of those
who do wrong; for like the grass they will soon wither, like green
plants they will soon die away.
PSALM 37:1–2 NIV

Commit your works to the LORD and your plans will be established.
The LORD has made everything for its own purpose, even the
wicked for the day of evil.
PROVERBS 16:3–4 NASB

Even though I walk through the darkest valley, I will fear no evil,
for you are with me; your rod and your staff, they comfort me.
PSALM 23:4 NIV

For you have made the LORD, my refuge, even the Most High, your
dwelling place. No evil will befall you, nor will any plague come
near your tent. For He will give His angels charge concerning
you, to guard you in all your ways.
PSALM 91:9–11 NASB

The person who bears and suffers evils with meekness and silence,
is the sum of a Christian man.
JOHN WESLEY

"Blessed are you when people insult you, persecute you and falsely say all kinds of evil against you because of me."
MATTHEW 5:11 NIV

"But I say to you, do not resist an evil person; but whoever slaps you on your right cheek, turn the other to him also."
MATTHEW 5:39 NASB

Repay no one evil for evil. Have regard for good things in the sight of all men.
ROMANS 12:17 NKJV

He who passively accepts evil is as much involved in it as he who helps to perpetrate it.
MARTIN LUTHER KING JR.

Set a watch, O LORD, before my mouth; keep the door of my lips. Incline not my heart to any evil thing, to practise wicked works with men that work iniquity: and let me not eat of their dainties.
PSALM 141:3–4 KJV

The LORD will keep you from all evil; he will keep your life. The LORD will keep your going out and your coming in from this time forth and forevermore.
PSALM 121:7–8 ESV

Those who believe that evil and the world are illusions do not actually function as if this were so. They may maintain that all is an illusion, but if one were to push them in front of an oncoming bus, they would quickly "warm up" to the reality idea!
NORMAN L. GEISLER

Do not be wise in your own eyes; fear the LORD and turn away from evil. It will be healing to your body and refreshment to your bones.
PROVERBS 3:7–8 NASB

He who earnestly seeks good finds favor,
but trouble will come to him who seeks evil.
PROVERBS 11:27 NKJV

> *It is not only that sin consists in doing evil,*
> *but in not doing the good that we know.*
> HARRY IRONSIDE

Do not be overcome by evil, but overcome evil with good.
ROMANS 12:21 NASB

Put everything to the test. Accept what is good and don't have anything to do with evil.
1 THESSALONIANS 5:21–22 CEV

Good people bring good things out of their hearts, but evil people bring evil things out of their hearts. I promise you that on the day of judgment, everyone will have to account for every careless word they have spoken.
MATTHEW 12:35–36 CEV

23

Faith

Faith is a wondrous thing. With it, we have the power to nurture children, the peace to calm hearts, the mind to think clearly, the heart to love entirely, the longing to pray, the soul to dream, and the spirit to serve. So take your faith and reach out to God. His response will be, "'Be of good cheer, daughter; your faith has made you well'" (Matthew 9:22 NKJV).

Trust in the LORD with all thine heart;
and lean not unto thine own understanding.
PROVERBS 3:5 KJV

It is by grace you have been saved, through faith—and this is not
from yourselves, it is the gift of God—not by works,
so that no one can boast.
EPHESIANS 2:8–9 NIV

Therefore, since we have been justified through faith, we have
peace with God through our Lord Jesus Christ, through whom
we have gained access by faith into this grace in which we now
stand. And we boast in the hope of the glory of God.
ROMANS 5:1–2 NIV

But that no one is justified by the law in the sight of God is
evident, for "the just shall live by faith."
GALATIANS 3:11 NKJV

*The beautiful thing about this adventure called faith is that we can
count on Him never to lead us astray.*
CHUCK SWINDOLL

Faith comes from hearing the message, and the message is
heard through the word about Christ.
ROMANS 10:17 NIV

Love the LORD, all his faithful people! The LORD preserves those
who are true to him, but the proud he pays back in full.
PSALM 31:23 NIV

Faith is two empty hands held open to receive all of the Lord.
ALAN REDPATH

Let love and faithfulness never leave you; bind them around your neck, write them on the tablet of your heart.

<small>Proverbs</small> 3:3 <small>niv</small>

The apostles said to the Lord, "Increase our faith!" And the Lord said, "If you had faith like a mustard seed, you would say to this mulberry tree, 'Be uprooted and be planted in the sea'; and it would obey you."

<small>Luke</small> 17:5–7 <small>nasb</small>

What though my body run to dust?
Faith cleaves unto it, counting ev'ry grain
With an exact and most particular trust.

<small>George Herbert</small>

You cannot make God accept you because of something you do. God accepts sinners only because they have faith in him.

<small>Romans</small> 4:5 <small>cev</small>

But now apart from the law the righteousness of God has been made known, to which the Law and the Prophets testify. This righteousness is given through faith in Jesus Christ to all who believe. There is no difference between Jew and Gentile, for all have sinned and fall short of the glory of God, and all are justified freely by his grace through the redemption that came by Christ Jesus.

<small>Romans</small> 3:21–24 <small>niv</small>

Faith is to believe what you do not yet see;
the reward for this faith is to see what you believe.

<small>Saint Augustine</small>

"We who are Jews by birth and not sinful Gentiles know that a person is not justified by the works of the law, but by faith in Jesus Christ. So we, too, have put our faith in Christ Jesus that we may be justified by faith in Christ and not by the works of the law, because by the works of the law no one will be justified."
GALATIANS 2:15–16 NIV

For we live by believing and not by seeing.
2 CORINTHIANS 5:7 NLT

"I have been crucified with Christ; and it is no longer I who live, but Christ lives in me; and the life which I now live in the flesh I live by faith in the Son of God, who loved me and gave Himself up for me."
GALATIANS 2:20 NASB

A true faith in Jesus Christ will not suffer us to be idle. No, it is an active, lively, restless principle; it fills the heart, so that it cannot be easy till it is doing something for Jesus Christ.
GEORGE WHITEFIELD

Even so faith, if it has no works, is dead, being by itself.
JAMES 2:17 NASB

Don't let anyone look down on you because you are young, but set an example for the believers in speech, in conduct, in love, in faith and in purity.
1 TIMOTHY 4:12 NIV

Watch, stand fast in the faith, be brave, be strong.
1 CORINTHIANS 16:13 NKJV

24

Fear

Some fear is healthy, like the fear of God. In that instance, fear means to revere with awe and respect. Any other fear comes from the dark side. God's Word frequently tells us we are not to fear but to trust Him. After all, if God is for us, who can be against us? So next time a spider crawls across your floor, don't panic. God is on your side! He'll crush your qualms.

Oh, that [the Hebrews] had such a heart in them that they would fear Me and always keep all My commandments, that it might be well with them and with their children forever!
DEUTERONOMY 5:29 NKJV

I have never once feared the devil,
but I tremble every time I enter the pulpit.
JOHN KNOX

"What does the LORD your God require of you, but to fear the LORD your God, to walk in all His ways and to love Him, to serve the LORD your God with all your heart and with all your soul, and to keep the commandments of the LORD and His statutes which I command you today for your good?"
DEUTERONOMY 10:12–13 NKJV

Yea, though I walk through the valley of the shadow of death, I will fear no evil: for thou art with me; thy rod and thy staff they comfort me.
PSALM 23:4 KJV

Though a host encamp against me, my heart will not fear; though war arise against me, in spite of this I shall be confident.
PSALM 27:3 NASB

I sought the LORD, and He heard me, and delivered me from all my fears.
PSALM 34:4 NKJV

Faith, which is trust, and fear are opposite poles. If a man has the one,
he can scarcely have the other in vigorous operation.
ALEXANDER MACLAREN

God is our refuge and strength, always ready to help in times of trouble. So we will not fear when earthquakes come and the mountains crumble into the sea. Let the oceans roar and foam. Let the mountains tremble as the waters surge!
PSALM 46:1–3 NLT

Are you facing fear today? . . . At times all of us experience fear. But don't allow fear to keep you from being used by God. He has kept you thus far; trust Him for the rest of the way.
WOODROW KROLL

Many. . .are pursuing and attacking me, but even when I am afraid, I keep on trusting you. I praise your promises! I trust you and am not afraid. No one can harm me.
PSALM 56:2–4 CEV

For all who are led by the Spirit of God are children of God. So you have not received a spirit that makes you fearful slaves. Instead, you received God's Spirit when he adopted you as his own children. Now we call him, "Abba, Father."
ROMANS 8:14–15 NLT

"And do not fear those who kill the body but cannot kill the soul. But rather fear Him who is able to destroy both soul and body in hell. Are not two sparrows sold for a copper coin? And not one of them falls to the ground apart from your Father's will. But the very hairs of your head are all numbered. Do not fear therefore; you are of more value than many sparrows."
MATTHEW 10:28–31 NKJV

For God has not given us a spirit of fear,
but of power and of love and of a sound mind.
2 TIMOTHY 1:7 NKJV

My little group of disciples, don't be afraid! Your Father wants to give you the kingdom. Sell what you have and give the money to the poor. Make yourselves moneybags that never wear out. Make sure your treasure is safe in heaven, where thieves cannot steal it and moths cannot destroy it.
LUKE 12:32–33 CEV

Fear is born of Satan, and if we would only take time to think a moment, we would see that everything Satan says is founded upon a falsehood.
A. B. SIMPSON

By faith [Moses] forsook Egypt, not fearing the wrath of the king; for he endured as seeing Him who is invisible.
HEBREWS 11:27 NKJV

Keep your lives free from the love of money and be content with what you have, because God has said, "Never will I leave you; never will I forsake you." So we say with confidence, "The Lord is my helper; I will not be afraid. What can mere mortals do to me?"
HEBREWS 13:5–6 NIV

There is no fear in love; but perfect love casts out fear, because fear involves punishment, and the one who fears is not perfected in love.
1 JOHN 4:18 NASB

When a man has quietly made up his mind that there is nothing he cannot endure, his fears leave him.
GROVE PATTERSON

25

Following God

Are you allowing God to navigate your life?
Or are you constantly ejecting Him from the
driver's seat and taking the wheel into your
own hands? God wants you to trust Him. So
let Him steer. You can peek over His shoulder
at the road map, but remember He's the best
GPS in the world! You don't always have to
know where you're going. Just have faith that
God is taking you in the right direction.

And now, Israel, what does the Lord your God ask of you but to fear the Lord your God, to walk in obedience to him, to love him, to serve the Lord your God with all your heart and with all your soul, and to observe the Lord's commands and decrees that I am giving you today for your own good?
Deuteronomy 10:12–13 NIV

God looks down from heaven on all mankind to see if there are any who understand, any who seek God.
Psalm 53:2 NIV

What were we made for? To know God. What aim should we have in life? To know God. What is the eternal life that Jesus gives? To know God. What is the best thing in life? To know God. What in humans gives God most pleasure? Knowledge of Himself.
J. I. Packer

Those who think they know something do not yet know as they ought to know. But whoever loves God is known by God.
1 Corinthians 8:2–3 NIV

Then Jesus spoke to them again, saying, "I am the light of the world. He who follows Me shall not walk in darkness, but have the light of life."
John 8:12 NKJV

The rule that governs my life is this: Anything that dims my vision of Christ, or takes away my taste for Bible study, or cramps my prayer life, or makes Christian work difficult, is wrong for me, and I must, as a Christian, turn away from it.
J. Wilbur Chapman

And thou shalt love the Lord thy God with all thy heart, and with all thy soul, and with all thy mind, and with all thy strength: this is the first commandment.
MARK 12:30 KJV

But now that you have come to know God, or rather to be known by God, how can you turn back again to the weak and worthless elementary principles of the world, whose slaves you want to be once more?
GALATIANS 4:9 ESV

If someone says, "I love God," and hates his brother, he is a liar; for he who does not love his brother whom he has seen, how can he love God whom he has not seen? And this commandment we have from Him: that he who loves God must love his brother also.
1 JOHN 4:20–21 NKJV

But if we live in the light, as God does, we share in life with each other. And the blood of his Son Jesus washes all our sins away.
1 JOHN 1:7 CEV

If I, an earthly father, can know such a sensation of pleasure in the well-being of my son, surely that gives an inkling of how our heavenly Father feels when we please Him. If we could only grasp and be grasped by this, our lives would be revolutionized.
ALISTAIR BEGG

"You shall follow the LORD your God and fear Him; and you shall keep His commandments, listen to His voice, serve Him, and cling to Him."
DEUTERONOMY 13:4 NASB

You have accepted Christ Jesus as your Lord.
Now keep on following him.
COLOSSIANS 2:6 CEV

So I say, walk by the Spirit, and you will not gratify
the desires of the flesh.
GALATIANS 5:16 NIV

And walk in love, as Christ also hath loved us, and hath
given himself for us an offering and a sacrifice to God for
a sweetsmelling savour.
EPHESIANS 5:2 KJV

We are his workmanship, created in Christ Jesus unto good works,
which God hath before ordained that we should walk in them.
EPHESIANS 2:10 KJV

The Christian ideal has not been tried and found wanting.
It has been found difficult and left untried.
G. K. CHESTERTON

26

Forgiveness

Women tend to hold grudges longer than men.
It's probably because we're more sensitive than
the average man. But there is hope. Through
God, His Word, and prayer, we can learn to
forgive—and forgive quickly. All we have
to do is remember how many times we've
wronged God and received His forgiveness.
Now have you got the right perspective?
Go. Forgive. Yeah, seven times seventy!

Who is a God like you, who pardons sin and forgives the transgression of the remnant of his inheritance? You do not stay angry forever but delight to show mercy. You will again have compassion on us; you will tread our sins underfoot and hurl all our iniquities into the depths of the sea.
MICAH 7:18–19 NIV

" 'The LORD is slow to anger, abounding in love and forgiving sin and rebellion. Yet he does not leave the guilty unpunished; he punishes the children for the sin of the parents to the third and fourth generation.' "
NUMBERS 14:18 NIV

If we are not humbled by the greatness of God's forgiveness, we need to question whether or not we have a relationship with Him.

"You are a forgiving God, gracious and compassionate, slow to anger and abounding in love."
NEHEMIAH 9:17 NIV

If my people, which are called by my name, shall humble themselves, and pray, and seek my face, and turn from their wicked ways; then will I hear from heaven, and will forgive their sin, and will heal their land.
2 CHRONICLES 7: 14 KJV

"He who is not with Me is against Me; and he who does not gather with Me scatters. Therefore I say to you, any sin and blasphemy shall be forgiven people, but blasphemy against the Spirit shall not be forgiven."
MATTHEW 12:30–31 NASB

Blessed is the one whose transgressions are forgiven,
whose sins are covered.
PSALM 32:1 NIV

God forgave us without any merit on our part; therefore we must
forgive others, whether or not we think they merit it.
LEHMAN STRAUSS

Bless the LORD, O my soul, and forget not all His benefits:
who forgives all your iniquities, who heals all your diseases,
who redeems your life from destruction, who crowns you with
lovingkindness and tender mercies.
PSALM 103:2–4 NKJV

If we confess our sins, he is faithful and just and will forgive
us our sins and purify us from all unrighteousness.
1 JOHN 1:9 NIV

For Your name's sake, O LORD, pardon my iniquity, for it is great.
PSALM 25:11 NKJV

"If you forgive other people when they sin against you, your
heavenly Father will also forgive you. But if you do not forgive
others their sins, your Father will not forgive your sins."
MATTHEW 6:14–15 NIV

We need not climb up into heaven to see whether our sins are forgiven:
let us look into our hearts, and see if we can forgive others.
If we can, we need not doubt but God has forgiven us.
THOMAS WATSON

Then Peter came to him and asked, "Lord, how often should I forgive someone who sins against me? Seven times?" "No, not seven times," Jesus replied, "but seventy times seven!"
MATTHEW 18:21–22 NLT

> *Forgiveness is an act of the will, and the will can function regardless of the temperature of the heart.*
> CORRIE TEN BOOM

"And when you stand praying, if you hold anything against anyone, forgive them, so that your Father in heaven may forgive you your sins."
MARK 11:25 NIV

"Take heed to yourselves. If your brother sins against you, rebuke him; and if he repents, forgive him. And if he sins against you seven times in a day, and seven times in a day returns to you, saying, 'I repent,' you shall forgive him."
LUKE 17:3–4 NKJV

> *A Christian will find it cheaper to pardon than resent. Forgiveness saves the expense of anger, the cost of hatred, the waste of spirits.*
> HANNAH MORE

When people sin, you should forgive and comfort them, so they won't give up in despair. You should make them sure of your love for them.
2 CORINTHIANS 2:7–8 CEV

Be kind and compassionate to one another, forgiving each other, just as in Christ God forgave you.
EPHESIANS 4:32 NIV

27

Friendship

A study has shown that unlike men, women have more than the flight-or-fight response when faced with stress. Instead, females find release in tending children or getting together with other women. So, ladies, cultivate and nurture those friendships. Doing so will enhance your inner peace, your relationship with the opposite sex, and your overall health.

The LORD would speak to Moses face to face,
as one speaks to a friend.
EXODUS 33:11 NIV

She also said, "But let me do one thing. Let me be alone for
two months to go to the mountains. Since I will never marry,
let me and my friends go and cry together."
JUDGES 11:37 NCV

*Lots of people want to ride with you in the limo, but what you want is
someone who will take the bus with you when the limo breaks down.*
OPRAH WINFREY

Three of Job's friends heard of all the trouble that had fallen on
him. Each traveled from his own country. . .and went together to
Job to keep him company and comfort him. . . . Seven days and
nights they sat there without saying a word. They could see how
rotten he felt, how deeply he was suffering.
JOB 2:11, 13 MSG

*Silences make the real conversations between friends.
Not the saying but the never needing to say is what counts.*
MARGARET LEE RUNBECK

"When I was in my prime, God's friendship was felt in my home."
JOB 29:4 NLT

When Job prayed for his friends, the LORD restored his fortunes.
In fact, the LORD gave him twice as much as before!
JOB 42:10 NLT

A true friend never gets in your way unless you happen to be going down.
ARNOLD H. GLASOW

Overlook an offense and bond a friendship;
fasten on to a slight and—good-bye, friend!
PROVERBS 17:9 MSG

Friends love through all kinds of weather, and families stick
together in all kinds of trouble.
PROVERBS 17:17 MSG

> *A friendship can weather most things and thrive in thin soil;*
> *but it needs a little mulch of letters and phone calls and small,*
> *silly presents every so often—just to save it from drying out completely.*
> PAM BROWN

There are "friends" who destroy each other, but a real friend
sticks closer than a brother.
PROVERBS 18:24 NLT

Wounds from a sincere friend are better than many kisses
from an enemy.
PROVERBS 27:6 NLT

Just as lotions and fragrance give sensual delight,
a sweet friendship refreshes the soul.
PROVERBS 27:9 MSG

You are better off to have a friend than to be all alone, because
then you will get more enjoyment out of what you earn. If you
fall, your friend can help you up. But if you fall without having a
friend nearby, you are really in trouble.
ECCLESIASTES 4:9–10 CEV

Dear friends, let us love one another, for love comes from God.
1 JOHN 4:7 NIV

"The Son of Man came eating and drinking, and you say, 'Look at him! He eats too much and drinks too much wine, and he is a friend of tax collectors and sinners!' "
LUKE 7:34 NCV

"And when she has found it, she calls her friends and neighbors together, saying, 'Rejoice with me, for I have found the piece which I lost!' "
LUKE 15:9 NKJV

It's the friends you can call up at 4 a.m. that matter.
MARLENE DIETRICH

"Greater love has no one than this: to lay down one's life for one's friends. You are my friends if you do what I command. I no longer call you servants, because a servant does not know his master's business. Instead, I have called you friends, for everything that I learned from my Father I have made known to you."
JOHN 15:13–15 NIV

Jesus, my Lord, thank You for being my best Friend,
for laying down Your life so I could live eternally.
Help me to love others as fully and truly as You love me.

And the Scripture was fulfilled which says, "Abraham believed God, and it was accounted to him for righteousness." And he was called the friend of God.
JAMES 2:23 NKJV

Walking with a friend in the dark is better
than walking alone in the light.
HELEN KELLER

28

Giving

Giving comes in all shapes and sizes, tangible
and intangible. There's the giving of time, money,
love, and service. But more important, there's
the giving of yourself. What are you giving each
and every day? You have received much from
God—love, salvation, grace, mercy. Are you
giving back? Remember, the more you give, the
more you receive in eternal and spiritual rewards!
So, give, girl, give! Bless and you will be blessed!

Give generously to them and do so without a grudging heart; then because of this the LORD your God will bless you in all your work and in everything you put your hand to.

DEUTERONOMY 15:10 NIV

Honor the LORD from your wealth and from the first of all your produce; so your barns will be filled with plenty and your vats will overflow with new wine.

PROVERBS 3:9–10 NASB

I am the LORD All-Powerful, and I challenge you to put me to the test. Bring the entire ten percent into the storehouse, so there will be food in my house. Then I will open the windows of heaven and flood you with blessing after blessing.

MALACHI 3:10 CEV

Make all you can, save all you can, give all you can.
JOHN WESLEY

"If there is among you a poor man of your brethren, within any of the gates in your land which the LORD your God is giving you, you shall not harden your heart nor shut your hand from your poor brother, but you shall open your hand wide to him and willingly lend him sufficient for his need, whatever he needs."

DEUTERONOMY 15:7–8 NKJV

There is one who scatters, yet increases more; and there is one who withholds more than is right, but it leads to poverty. The generous soul will be made rich, and he who waters will also be watered himself.

PROVERBS 11:24–25 NKJV

The best way to do ourselves good is to be doing good to others;
the best way to gather is to scatter.
THOMAS BROOKS

If you give to others, you will be given a full amount in return.
It will be packed down, shaken together, and spilling over into
your lap. The way you treat others is the way you will be treated.
LUKE 6:38 CEV

Remember that our Lord Jesus said, "More blessings come from
giving than from receiving."
ACTS 20:35 CEV

You can't have a perfect day without doing something
for someone who'll never be able to repay you.
JOHN WOODEN

"O our God. . .everything we have has come from you,
and we give you only what you first gave us!"
1 CHRONICLES 29:13–14 NLT

Each of you has received a gift to use to serve others.
Be good servants of God's various gifts of grace.
1 PETER 4:10 NCV

If your gift is to encourage others, be encouraging. If it is giving,
give generously. If God has given you leadership ability, take
the responsibility seriously. And if you have a gift for showing
kindness to others, do it gladly.
ROMANS 12:8 NLT

Be generous, and someday you will be rewarded.
ECCLESIASTES 11:1 CEV

Some people give time, some money, some their skills and connections,
some literally give their life's blood. But everyone has something to give.
BARBARA BUSH

If you feed those who are hungry and take care of the needs of
those who are troubled, then your light will shine in the darkness,
and you will be bright like sunshine at noon.
ISAIAH 58:10 NCV

It is possible to give without loving,
but it is impossible to love without giving.
RICHARD BRAUNSTEIN

It doesn't matter how much you have. What matters is how much
you are willing to give from what you have.
2 CORINTHIANS 8:12 CEV

If you can't feed a hundred people, then just feed one.
MOTHER TERESA

On the first day of every week, each one of you should put aside
money as you have been blessed.
1 CORINTHIANS 16:2 NCV

"When you do a charitable deed, do not let your left hand know
what your right hand is doing, that your charitable deed may be
in secret; and your Father who sees in secret will Himself
reward you openly."
MATTHEW 6:3–4 NKJV

To give without reward, or any notice, has a special quality of its own.
ANNE MORROW LINDBERGH

29
God's Love

The love of God is unfathomable and unlimited.
Although husbands, lovers, sisters, brothers,
children, friends, and others may reject or
hurt you—intentionally or unintentionally—
God will not. No matter what you do, He
will not desert you. With gentle hands, He
will bind up your wounds and examine your
scars. Immerse yourself in God's love. As
He fills you to overflowing within, turn and
lavish that love upon others without.

"For God so loved the world that He gave His only begotten Son, that whoever believes in Him should not perish but have everlasting life."

JOHN 3:16 NKJV

The Cross is the ultimate evidence that there is no length the love of God will refuse to go in effecting reconciliation.

R. KENT HUGHES

Then the LORD came down in the cloud and stood there with him and proclaimed his name, the LORD. And he passed in front of Moses, proclaiming, "The LORD, the LORD, the compassionate and gracious God, slow to anger, abounding in love and faithfulness, maintaining love to thousands, and forgiving wickedness, rebellion and sin. Yet he does not leave the guilty unpunished; he punishes the children and their children for the sin of the parents to the third and fourth generation."

EXODUS 34:5–7 NIV

"Understand, therefore, that the LORD your God is indeed God. He is the faithful God who keeps his covenant for a thousand generations and lavishes his unfailing love on those who love him and obey his commands."

DEUTERONOMY 7:9 NLT

Thank GOD! He deserves your thanks. His love never quits. Thank the God of all gods, His love never quits. Thank the Lord of all lords. His love never quits.

PSALM 136:2 MSG

"The LORD your God is with you, the Mighty Warrior who saves. He will take great delight in you; in his love he will no longer rebuke you, but will rejoice over you with singing."

ZEPHANIAH 3:17 NIV

"The Father Himself loves you, because you have loved Me and have believed that I came forth from the Father."
JOHN 16:27 NASB

We keep asking, "Who am I that the Lord should love me?"
Instead we ought to be asking, "Who are you, O my God,
that You love me so much?"
JOHN POWELL

But I am like an olive tree, thriving in the house of God.
I will always trust in God's unfailing love.
PSALM 52:8 NLT

The cross is the lightning rod of grace that short-circuits God's wrath
to Christ so that only the light of His love remains for believers.
A. W. TOZER

And hope does not put us to shame, because God's love has been poured out into our hearts through the Holy Spirit, who has been given to us. You see, at just the right time, when we were still powerless, Christ died for the ungodly. Very rarely will anyone die for a righteous person, though for a good person someone might possibly dare to die. But God demonstrates his own love for us in this: While we were still sinners, Christ died for us.
ROMANS 5:5–8 NIV

Nothing in all creation can separate us from God's love for us in Christ Jesus our Lord!
ROMANS 8:39 CEV

This is love: not that we loved God, but that he loved us and sent his Son as an atoning sacrifice for our sins.
1 JOHN 4:10 NIV

If we comprehend what Christ has done for us, then surely out of
gratitude we will strive to live "worthy" of such great love.
We will strive for holiness not to make God love us
but because He already does.
PHILIP YANCEY

Therefore be imitators of God as dear children. And walk in love,
as Christ also has loved us and given Himself for us, an offering
and a sacrifice to God for a sweet-smelling aroma.
EPHESIANS 5:1–3 NKJV

Behold what manner of love the Father has bestowed on us,
that we should be called children of God!
1 JOHN 3:1 NKJV

When God calls a man, He does not repent of it. God does not,
as many friends do, love one day, and hate another. . . .
Acts of grace cannot be reversed. God blots out
His people's sins, but not their names.
THOMAS WATSON

No one has seen God at any time; if we love one another,
God abides in us, and His love is perfected in us.
1 JOHN 4:12 NASB

We have come to know and have believed the love which God
has for us. God is love, and the one who abides in love abides
in God, and God abides in him.
1 JOHN 4:16 NASB

30
God's Will

Women are planners. We like to know where
we're going, when, and why. But life is full of
unscheduled events, interruptions, dead ends,
and U-turns—all within God's will. So relax,
ladies. Put your trust in the One who holds
the world in His hands. Seek His will through
prayer and His Word. Be open to the detours
God puts in your life as you move forward,
step- by-step. He'll get you where you need to be.

"Remain in me, as I also remain in you. No branch can bear fruit by itself; it must remain in the vine. Neither can you bear fruit unless you remain in me. I am the vine; you are the branches. If you remain in me and I in you, you will bear much fruit; apart from me you can do nothing."

JOHN 15:4–5 NIV

In Him we have redemption through His blood, the forgiveness of sins, according to the riches of His grace which He made to abound toward us in all wisdom and prudence, having made known to us the mystery of His will, according to His good pleasure which He purposed in Himself, that in the dispensation of the fullness of the times He might gather together in one all things in Christ, both which are in heaven and which are on earth—in Him.

EPHESIANS 1:7–10 NKJV

"And you must love the LORD your God with all your heart, all your soul, and all your strength."

DEUTERONOMY 6:5 NLT

"You must not have any other god but me."

EXODUS 20:3 NLT

We discover the will of God by a sensitive application
of scripture to our own lives.
SINCLAIR FERGUSON

Therefore, my dear friends, as you have always obeyed. . . continue to work out your salvation with fear and trembling, for it is God who works in you to will and to act in order to fulfill his good purpose.

PHILIPPIANS 2:12–13 NIV

Trust in the LORD with all your heart,
and lean not on your own understanding.
PROVERBS 3:5 NKJV

*Abide in Jesus, the sinless One—which means, give up all of self
and its life, and dwell in God's will and rest in His strength.
This is what brings the power that does not commit sin.*
ANDREW MURRAY

And do not be conformed to this world, but be transformed by
the renewing of your mind, so that you may prove what the will
of God is, that which is good and acceptable and perfect.
ROMANS 12:2 NASB

I urge, then, first of all, that petitions, prayers, intercession and
thanksgiving be made for all people—for kings and all those
in authority, that we may live peaceful and quiet lives in all godliness
and holiness. This is good, and pleases God our Savior, who wants
all people to be saved and to come to a knowledge of the truth.
1 TIMOTHY 2:1–4 NIV

Be devoted to one another in brotherly love; give preference to
one another in honor; not lagging behind in diligence, fervent
in spirit, serving the Lord; rejoicing in hope, persevering in
tribulation, devoted to prayer.
ROMANS 12:10–12 NASB

Be very careful, then, how you live—not as unwise but as wise,
making the most of every opportunity, because the days are evil.
Therefore do not be foolish, but understand what the Lord's will
is. Do not get drunk on wine, which leads to debauchery. Instead,
be filled with the Spirit.
EPHESIANS 5:15–18 NIV

Proceed with much prayer, and your way will be made plain.
JOHN WESLEY

Commit your works to the LORD,
and your thoughts will be established.
PROVERBS 16:3 NKJV

God's will is for you to be holy, so stay away from all sexual sin.
1 THESSALONIANS 4:3 NLT

*We must know that as His children, He's going to allow
problems even when we are in the center of His will.*
SANDY EDMONSON

If you need wisdom, ask our generous God, and he will give it to
you. He will not rebuke you for asking.
JAMES 1:5 NLT

For it is God's will that by doing good you should silence the
ignorant talk of foolish people.
1 PETER 2:15 NIV

31
God's Word

God spoke and the world came into being.
Now that's power! There's power in His Word!
Are you in it? Daily seek God's presence,
Son, Spirit, and guidance in the Bible. Allow
it to nurture you as you nurture others.
Doing so will give you strength, direction,
fulfillment, and a positive, eternal perspective
as you focus on and learn about God. And
memorizing scripture will give you power
against the darkness. Woman, Word up!

By the word of God the heavens were of old, and the earth standing out of water and in the water, by which the world that then existed perished, being flooded with water.
2 Peter 3:5–6 nkjv

> *Too often, we look to the Bible as our guidebook for daily living. Of course, that's fine and even biblical. However, this collection of books we call the Holy Bible is much more than a self-help book. The divine purpose of this book is to point us to the One and Only.*
> Randy Hunt

The Word was first, the Word present to God, God present to the Word. The Word was God, in readiness for God from day one.
John 1:1–2 msg

So the Word became human and made his home among us. He was full of unfailing love and faithfulness. And we have seen his glory, the glory of the Father's one and only Son.
John 1:14 nlt

The Son is the radiance of God's glory and the exact representation of his being, sustaining all things by his powerful word. After he had provided purification for sins, he sat down at the right hand of the Majesty in heaven.
Hebrews 1:3 niv

The word of the Lord is right and true; he is faithful in all he does.
Psalm 33:4 niv

All Scripture is God-breathed and is useful for teaching, rebuking, correcting and training in righteousness, so that the servant of God may be thoroughly equipped for every good work.
2 Timothy 3:16–17 niv

"Have faith in me, and you will have life-giving water flowing from deep inside you, just as the Scriptures say."
JOHN 7:38 CEV

> *The Bible cannot be understood simply by study or talent;*
> *you must count only on the influence of the Holy Spirit.*
> MARTIN LUTHER

Above all, you must realize that no prophecy in Scripture ever came from the prophet's own understanding, or from human initiative. No, those prophets were moved by the Holy Spirit, and they spoke from God.
2 PETER 1:20–21 NLT

> *The Bible is a window in this prison of hope,*
> *through which we look into eternity.*
> JOHN SULLIVAN DWIGHT

So get rid of all the filth and evil in your lives, and humbly accept the word God has planted in your hearts, for it has the power to save your souls. But don't just listen to God's word. You must do what it says. Otherwise, you are only fooling yourselves. For if you listen to the word and don't obey, it is like glancing at your face in a mirror.
JAMES 1:21–23 NLT

I have written to you who are God's children because you know the Father. I have written to you who are mature in the faith because you know Christ, who existed from the beginning. I have written to you who are young in the faith because you are strong. God's word lives in your hearts, and you have won your battle with the evil one.
1 JOHN 2:14 NLT

Whoever says, "I know him," but does not do what he commands is a liar, and the truth is not in that person. But if anyone obeys his word, love for God is truly made complete in them. This is how we know we are in him: Whoever claims to live in him must live as Jesus did.

1 JOHN 2:4–6 NIV

> *Defend the Bible? I would just as soon defend a lion.*
> *Just turn the Bible loose. It will defend itself.*
> C. H. SPURGEON

But the Scripture has shut up everyone under sin, so that the promise by faith in Jesus Christ might be given to those who believe.

GALATIANS 3:22 NASB

After he was raised from the dead, his disciples recalled what he had said. Then they believed the scripture and the words that Jesus had spoken.

JOHN 2:22 NIV

For, "All people are like grass, and all their glory is like the flowers of the field; the grass withers and the flowers fall, but the word of the Lord endures forever." And this is the word that was preached to you.

1 PETER 1:24–25 NIV

Thy word is a lamp unto my feet, and a light unto my path.

PSALM 119:105 KJV

Forever, O LORD, your word is firmly fixed in the heavens.

PSALM 119:89 ESV

32
Grace

Grace isn't just something mothers teach their
children to pray before meals. It's so much more.
Grace is the inexhaustible forgiveness, infinite
loving-kindness, and unfathomable mercy God
bestows on us—all personified in God's Son,
Jesus. Because God has bestowed such amazing
grace on us, we are enabled to treat others with
grace and forgiveness. Grace—how divine!

And he passed in front of Moses, proclaiming, "The LORD,
the LORD, the compassionate and gracious God, slow to anger,
abounding in love and faithfulness, maintaining love to thousands,
and forgiving wickedness, rebellion and sin."
EXODUS 34:6–7 NIV

For this reason it is by faith, in order that it may be in accordance
with grace, so that the promise will be guaranteed to all the
descendants, not only to those who are of the Law,
but also to those who are of the faith of Abraham,
who is the father of us all.
ROMANS 4:16 NASB

Let us then fearlessly and confidently and boldly draw near to
the throne of grace (the throne of God's unmerited favor to us
sinners), that we may receive mercy [for our failures] and find
grace to help in good time for every need [appropriate help and
well-timed help, coming just when we need it].
HEBREWS 4:16 AMP

> *Grace is available for each of us every day—our spiritual daily
> bread—but we've got to remember to ask for it with a grateful heart
> and not worry about whether there will be enough for tomorrow.*
> SARAH BAN BREATHNACH

So the Word became human and made his home among us.
He was full of unfailing love and faithfulness. . . . From his
abundance we have all received one gracious blessing after
another. For the law was given through Moses, but God's
unfailing love and faithfulness came through Jesus Christ.
JOHN 1:14, 16–17 NLT

All of us have sinned and fallen short of God's glory. But God treats us much better than we deserve, and because of Christ Jesus, he freely accepts us and sets us free from our sins.
Romans 3:23–24 CEV

Being made right with God by his grace, we could have the hope of receiving the life that never ends.
Titus 3:7 NCV

Lord, I bow before You in appreciation of the unlimited grace You have bestowed upon me. As my spirit drinks in Your unmerited favor, let it overflow out of me and onto others.

We have different gifts, according to the grace given to each of us.
Romans 12:6 NIV

Through [Jesus] we have received grace and apostleship for obedience to the faith among all nations for His name.
Romans 1:5 NKJV

In [Jesus] we have redemption through his blood, the forgiveness of sins, in accordance with the riches of God's grace that he lavished on us.
Ephesians 1:7–8 NIV

But He gives us more and more grace (power of the Holy Spirit, to meet this evil tendency and all others fully). That is why He says, God sets Himself against the proud and haughty, but gives grace [continually] to the lowly (those who are humble enough to receive it).
James 4:6 AMP

Likewise you younger people, submit yourselves to your elders. Yes, all of you be submissive to one another, and be clothed with humility, for "God resists the proud, but gives grace to the humble."
1 PETER 5:5 NKJV

For by grace are ye saved through faith; and that not of yourselves: it is the gift of God.
EPHESIANS 2:8 KJV

You are so weak. Give up to grace.
The ocean takes care of each wave
till it gets to shore.
JALAL AD-DIN RUMI

Don't be selfish; don't try to impress others. Be humble, thinking of others as better than yourselves. Don't look out only for your own interests, but take an interest in others, too.
PHILIPPIANS 2:3–4 NLT

And you know, when you've experienced grace and you feel like you've
been forgiven, you're a lot more forgiving of other people.
You're a lot more gracious to others.
RICK WARREN

Let your conversation be always full of grace, seasoned with salt, so that you may know how to answer everyone.
COLOSSIANS 4:6 NIV

Let the wonderful kindness and the understanding that come from our Lord and Savior Jesus Christ help you to keep on growing. Praise Jesus now and forever! Amen.
2 PETER 3:18 CEV

All grace grows as love to the Word of God grows.
PHILIP HENRY

That is the way we should live, because God's grace that can save everyone has come. It teaches us not to live against God nor to do the evil things the world wants to do. Instead, that grace teaches us to live in the present age in a wise and right way and in a way that shows we serve God.
TITUS 2:11–12 NCV

I do not at all understand the mystery of grace—only that it meets us where we are but does not leave us where it found us.
ANNE LAMOTT

The grace of our Lord Jesus Christ be with you all. Amen.
2 THESSALONIANS 3:18 KJV

33

Grief

When we've suffered the loss of a job, a divorce,
our ability to bear children, the demise of a loved
one, or some other hardship, we encounter the
sometimes concurrent stages of grief—denial,
anger, bargaining, depression, and acceptance.
And just when we think we're out of the muck,
we're mired in sadness again. The good news?
Jesus, who suffered everything we have, is ready
to take us in His arms, comfort us, give us hope.
Hang on, sister. Jesus will see you through.

The LORD is my shepherd. . . . He maketh me to lie down in green pastures: he leadeth me beside the still waters. He restoreth my soul. . . . Yea, though I walk through the valley of the shadow of death, I will fear no evil: for thou art with me; thy rod and thy staff they comfort me.
PSALM 23:1–4 KJV

Weeping may endure for a night, but joy comes in the morning.
PSALM 30:5 NKJV

Tears are God's gift to us. Our holy water. They heal us as they flow.
RITA SCHIANO

The LORD is near to the brokenhearted and saves those who are crushed in spirit.
PSALM 34:18 NASB

God can heal a broken heart, but He has to have all the pieces.
UNKNOWN

God is our refuge and strength, an ever-present help in trouble. Therefore we will not fear, though the earth give way and the mountains fall into the heart of the sea.
PSALM 46:1–2 NIV

There are things that we don't want to happen but have to accept, things we don't want to know but have to learn, and people we can't live without but have to let go.
UNKNOWN

"You're blessed when you feel you've lost what is most dear to you. Only then can you be embraced by the One most dear to you."
MATTHEW 5:4 MSG

You have allowed me to suffer much hardship, but you will restore me to life again and lift me up from the depths of the earth. You will restore me to even greater honor and comfort me once again.
PSALM 71:20–21 NLT

Those who hope in the LORD will renew their strength. They will soar on wings like eagles; they will run and not grow weary, they will walk and not be faint.
ISAIAH 40:31 NIV

Sadness flies away on the wings of time.
JEAN DE LA FONTAINE

"I will comfort you there like a mother comforting her child.". . . You will celebrate; your strength will return faster than grass can sprout. Then everyone will know that the LORD is present with his servants.
ISAIAH 66:13–14 CEV

Joy comes, grief goes, we know not how.
JAMES RUSSELL LOWELL

For no one is abandoned by the Lord forever. Though he brings grief, he also shows compassion because of the greatness of his unfailing love. For he does not enjoy hurting people or causing them sorrow.
LAMENTATIONS 3:31–33 NLT

"Come to me, all you who are weary and burdened, and I will give you rest."
MATTHEW 11:28 NIV

When you are sorrowful, look again in your heart, and you shall see that in truth you are weeping for that which has been your delight.
KHALIL GIBRAN

God is the Father who is full of mercy and all comfort. He comforts us every time we have trouble, so when others have trouble, we can comfort them with the same comfort God gives us. We share in the many sufferings of Christ. In the same way, much comfort comes to us through Christ.
2 CORINTHIANS 1:3–5 NCV

So we do not give up. Our physical body is becoming older and weaker, but our spirit inside us is made new every day.
2 CORINTHIANS 4:16 NCV

My grace is enough; it's all you need. My strength comes into its own in your weakness.
2 CORINTHIANS 12:9 MSG

[Jesus] understands our weaknesses, for he faced all of the same testings we do, yet he did not sin. So let us come boldly to the throne of our gracious God. There we will receive his mercy, and we will find grace to help us when we need it most.
HEBREWS 4:15–16 NLT

Humble yourselves, therefore, under God's mighty hand, that he may lift you up in due time. Cast all your anxiety on him because he cares for you.
1 PETER 5:6–7 NIV

34

Healing

The Bible is full of examples of named and
unnamed women who were healed immediately
or over time. God restored them not only
physically but spiritually, financially, emotionally,
mentally, relationally, and more. Jesus healed
not only these women but their loved ones
as well—sons, husbands, mothers, sisters,
daughters, and in-laws. Our compassionate
God is ready, willing, and able to make us whole
again. All we need is faith, a fervent prayer,
and a willingness to wait for God's timing.

Then Abraham prayed to God, and God healed Abimelek,
his wife and his female slaves so they could have children again.
GENESIS 20:17 NIV

The soul is healed by being with children.
FYODOR DOSTOYEVSKY

"I have heard your prayer, I have seen your tears;
behold, I will heal you."
2 KINGS 20:5 NASB

Have mercy on me, O LORD, for I am weak;
O LORD, heal me, for my bones are troubled.
PSALM 6:2 NKJV

He heals the brokenhearted and bandages their wounds.
PSALM 147:3 NCV

All healing is first a healing of the heart.
CARL TOWNSEND

For everything there is a season. . . . A time to kill and a time to
heal. A time to tear down and a time to build up.
ECCLESIASTES 3:1, 3 NLT

They will come back to the LORD, and he will listen to their
prayers and heal them.
ISAIAH 19:22 NCV

"LORD, heal me, and I will truly be healed. Save me, and I will truly
be saved. You are the one I praise."
JEREMIAH 17:14 NCV

"I have seen what they have done, but I will heal them. I will guide them and comfort them and those who felt sad for them. They will all praise me. I will give peace, real peace, to those far and near, and I will heal them," says the Lord.
ISAIAH 57:18–19 NCV

But he was wounded for the wrong we did; he was crushed for the evil we did. The punishment, which made us well, was given to him, and we are healed because of his wounds.
ISAIAH 53:5 NCV

Then Jesus said to the officer, "You may go home now. Your faith has made it happen." Right then his servant was healed.
MATTHEW 8:13 CEV

All who call on God in true faith, earnestly from the heart, will certainly be heard, and will receive what they have asked and desired.
MARTIN LUTHER

Jesus went to the home of Peter, where he found that Peter's mother-in-law was sick in bed with fever. He took her by the hand, and the fever left her. Then she got up and served Jesus a meal.
MATTHEW 8:14–15 CEV

Just then a woman who had suffered for twelve years with constant bleeding. . .touched the fringe of his robe, for she thought, "If I can just touch his robe, I will be healed." Jesus turned around, and when he saw her he said, "Daughter, be encouraged! Your faith has made you well." And the woman was healed at that moment.
MATTHEW 9:20–22 NLT

"Heal the sick, raise the dead, cure those with leprosy, and cast out demons. Give as freely as you have received!"
MATTHEW 10:8 NLT

The greatest healing therapy is friendship and love.
HUBERT H. HUMPHREY

[Jesus] took his twelve disciples with him, along with some women who had been cured of evil spirits and diseases. Among them were Mary Magdalene, from whom he had cast out seven demons; Joanna, the wife of Chuza, Herod's business manager; Susanna; and many others.
LUKE 8:1–3 NLT

All the people were trying to touch Jesus, because power was coming from him and healing them all.
LUKE 6:19 NCV

I had no idea that mothering my own child would be so healing to my own sadness from my childhood.
SUSIE BRIGHT

Confess to one another therefore your faults (your slips, your false steps, your offenses, your sins) and pray [also] for one another, that you may be healed and restored [to a spiritual tone of mind and heart]. The earnest (heartfelt, continued) prayer of a righteous man makes tremendous power available [dynamic in its working].
JAMES 5:16 AMP

To heal from the inside out is the key.
WYNONNA JUDD

35
Health

Singing "I'm a Woman," Bette Midler touts the talents of female multitaskers: "I can. . .feed the baby, grease the car, and powder my face at the same time"! Having a busy schedule is okay, as long as you're not neglecting yourself or God. Make sure you eat right, exercise daily, get enough rest, and spend time with the Lord. He'll help you do whatever you need to do today. Leave the rest for tomorrow.

"Six days you shall labor and do all your work, but the seventh day is a sabbath to the LORD your God. On it you shall not do any work, neither you, nor your son or daughter, nor your male or female servant, nor your animals, nor any foreigner residing in your towns."
EXODUS 20:9–10 NIV

Rest when you're weary. Refresh and renew yourself, your body, your mind, your spirit. Then get back to work.
RALPH MARSTON

Listen carefully to my words. Don't lose sight of them. Let them penetrate deep into your heart, for they bring life to those who find them, and healing to their whole body. Guard your heart above all else, for it determines the course of your life.
PROVERBS 4:20–23 NLT

You, LORD, are my shepherd. I will never be in need. You let me rest in fields of green grass. You lead me to streams of peaceful water, and you refresh my life.
PSALM 23:1–3 CEV

Come unto me, all ye that labour and are heavy laden, and I will give you rest. Take my yoke upon you, and learn of me; for I am meek and lowly in heart: and ye shall find rest unto your souls.
MATTHEW 11:28–29 KJV

We should do our best to enter that place of rest, so that none of us will disobey and miss going there.
HEBREWS 4:11 CEV

Sometimes the most urgent thing you can possibly do is take a complete rest.
ASHLEIGH BRILLIANT

I lie down and sleep; I wake again, because the Lord sustains me.
Psalm 3:5 niv

Dear friend, guard Clear Thinking and Common Sense with your life; don't for a minute lose sight of them. They'll keep your soul alive and well, they'll keep you fit and attractive.
Proverbs 3:21–22 msg

[The Lord] said to me, "My grace is sufficient for you, for my power is made perfect in weakness." Therefore I will boast all the more gladly about my weaknesses, so that Christ's power may rest on me. . . . For when I am weak, then I am strong.
2 Corinthians 12:9–10 niv

In peace I will lie down and sleep, for you alone,
Lord, make me dwell in safety.
Psalm 4:8 niv

Know, then, whatever cheerful and serene
Supports the mind supports the body, too.
John Armstrong

Health and cheerfulness naturally beget each other.
Joseph Addison

" 'Behold, I will bring to it health and healing, and I will heal them; and I will reveal to them an abundance of peace and truth.' "
Jeremiah 33:6 nasb

Exercise daily in God—no spiritual flabbiness, please! Workouts in the gymnasium are useful, but a disciplined life in God is far more so, making you fit both today and forever. You can count on this.
1 Timothy 4:8–9 msg

Don't drink too much wine and get drunk; don't eat too much food and get fat. Drunks and gluttons will end up on skid row, in a stupor and dressed in rags.
PROVERBS 23:20–21 MSG

A cheerful heart is good medicine,
but a crushed spirit dries up the bones.
PROVERBS 17:22 NIV

*When it comes to eating right and exercising,
there is no "I'll start tomorrow." Tomorrow is disease.*
TERRI GUILLEMETS

So I went to the angel and asked him to give me the little scroll. He said to me, "Take it and eat it."
REVELATION 10:9 NIV

Truly my soul finds rest in God; my salvation comes from him. . . . Yes, my soul, find rest in God; my hope comes from him.
PSALM 62:1, 5 NIV

Confidence and hope do more good than physic.
GALEN

Beloved, I pray that you may prosper in all things and be in health, just as your soul prospers.
3 JOHN 1:2 NKJV

We take our lead from Christ, who is the source of everything we do. He keeps us in step with each other. His very breath and blood flow through us, nourishing us so that we will grow up healthy in God, robust in love.
EPHESIANS 4:15–16 MSG

36
Holy Spirit

When Jesus left earth, He sent us the Holy Spirit—a Friend to comfort and guide us. Residing within us, He fills us with His presence, empowering us to do the impossible. Like the Spirit-filled Elizabeth—who loudly proclaimed to Mary, " 'Blessed is she who has believed that the Lord would fulfill his promises to her!' " (Luke 1:45 NIV)—we, too, can influence our families and communities for Jesus. Now that's empowerment!

"But the Helper, the Holy Spirit, whom the Father will send in My name, He will teach you all things, and bring to your remembrance all things that I said to you."
JOHN 14:26 NKJV

Again Jesus said, "Peace be with you! As the Father has sent me, I am sending you." And with that he breathed on them and said, "Receive the Holy Spirit."
JOHN 20:21–23 NIV

I tell you that any sinful thing you do or say can be forgiven. Even if you speak against the Son of Man, you can be forgiven. But if you speak against the Holy Spirit, you can never be forgiven, either in this life or in the life to come.
MATTHEW 12:32 CEV

Christ died to heal our relationship with God, but the Holy Spirit enables us to live for Him. Our relationship is with the Father, Son, and Holy Spirit, and in our lives each works in concert with the other persons of the Trinity.

"If you then, being evil, know how to give good gifts to your children, how much more will your heavenly Father give the Holy Spirit to those who ask Him?"
LUKE 11:13 NASB

"Therefore go and make disciples of all nations, baptizing them in the name of the Father and of the Son and of the Holy Spirit, and teaching them to obey everything I have commanded you. And surely I am with you always, to the very end of the age."
MATTHEW 28:19–20 NIV

"When you are brought before synagogues, rulers and authorities, do not worry about how you will defend yourselves or what you will say, for the Holy Spirit will teach you at that time what you should say."
LUKE 12:11–13 NIV

And they were all filled with the Holy Spirit and began to speak in other tongues as the Spirit gave them utterance.
ACTS 2:4 ESV

Without the Spirit of God, we can do nothing. We are as ships without wind or chariots without steeds. Like branches without sap, we are withered. Like coals without fire, we are useless. As an offering without the sacrificial flame, we are unaccepted.
C. H. SPURGEON

The church then had peace throughout Judea, Galilee, and Samaria, and it became stronger as the believers lived in the fear of the Lord. And with the encouragement of the Holy Spirit, it also grew in numbers.
ACTS 9:31 NLT

He chose me to be a servant of Christ Jesus for the Gentiles and to do the work of a priest in the service of his good news. God did this so that the Holy Spirit could make the Gentiles into a holy offering, pleasing to him.
ROMANS 15:16 CEV

Trying to do the Lord's work in your own strength is the most confusing, exhausting, and tedious of all work. But when you are filled with the Holy Spirit, then the ministry of Jesus just flows out of you.
CORRIE TEN BOOM

Paul and his companions traveled throughout the region of Phrygia and Galatia, having been kept by the Holy Spirit from preaching the word in the province of Asia. When they came to the border of Mysia, they tried to enter Bithynia, but the Spirit of Jesus would not allow them to.

ACTS 16:6–7 NIV

As they ministered to the Lord and fasted, the Holy Spirit said, "Now separate to Me Barnabas and Saul for the work to which I have called them."

ACTS 13:2 NKJV

In any matter where we have questions, we have a right to ask the Holy Spirit to lead us and to expect His gentle guiding.

CURTIS HUTSON

Now hope does not disappoint, because the love of God has been poured out in our hearts by the Holy Spirit who was given to us.

ROMANS 5:5 NKJV

Do not cast me away from Your presence and do not take Your Holy Spirit from me.

PSALM 51:11 NASB

Do you not know that your bodies are temples of the Holy Spirit, who is in you, whom you have received from God? You are not your own; you were bought at a price. Therefore honor God with your bodies.

1 CORINTHIANS 6:19–20 NIV

Don't let obstacles along the road to eternity shake your confidence in God's promise. The Holy Spirit is God's seal that you will arrive.

DAVID JEREMIAH

37
Hope

Need a power lift? Things looking desperate
in these troubled times? Put your hope in
God. He will never let you down. Be like
Deborah, a mother of Israel. Even when
her commander let her down, she kept her
hope in God and obtained a great victory
for herself, her God, and her people.

"Though He slay me, I will hope in Him."
JOB 13:15 NASB

No one who hopes in you will ever be put to shame, but shame
will come on those who are treacherous without cause.
PSALM 25:3 NIV

> *"Tribulation worketh patience; and patience, experience;
> and experience, hope." That is the order. You cannot put patience
> and experience into a parenthesis, and, omitting them,
> bring hope out of tribulation.*
> ALEXANDER MACLAREN

We glory in tribulations also: knowing that tribulation worketh
patience; and patience, experience; and experience, hope:
and hope maketh not ashamed; because the love of God is shed
abroad in our hearts by the Holy Ghost which is given unto us.
ROMANS 5:3–5 KJV

Lead me by your truth and teach me, for you are the God who
saves me. All day long I put my hope in you.
PSALM 25:5 NLT

> *As far as the Lord is concerned, the time to stand is in the darkest
> moment. It is when everything seems hopeless, when there appears
> no way out, when God alone can deliver.*
> DAVID WILKERSON

Why, my soul, are you downcast? Why so disturbed within me?
Put your hope in God, for I will yet praise him,
my Savior and my God.
PSALM 42:11 NIV

Hope deferred makes the heart sick,
but a dream fulfilled is a tree of life.
PROVERBS 13:12 NLT

For God alone, O my soul, wait in silence,
for my hope is from him.
PSALM 62:5 ESV

> *If you have any hope, it comes from some faith in you.*
> *Hope, you may say, is a bud upon the plant of faith,*
> *a bud from the root of faith; the flower is joy and peace.*
> GEORGE MACDONALD

Hopes placed in mortals die with them;
all the promise of their power comes to nothing.
PROVERBS 11:7 NIV

> *If we go forth in our own strength, we shall faint, and utterly fall;*
> *but having our hearts and our hopes in heaven, we shall be carried*
> *above all difficulties, and be enabled to lay hold of the prize of*
> *our high calling in Christ Jesus.*
> MATTHEW HENRY

Even youths grow tired and weary, and young men stumble and
fall; but those who hope in the LORD will renew their strength.
They will soar on wings like eagles; they will run and not grow
weary, they will walk and not be faint.
ISAIAH 40:30–31 NIV

Instruct those who are rich in this present world not to be
conceited or to fix their hope on the uncertainty of riches,
but on God, who richly supplies us with all things to enjoy.
1 TIMOTHY 6:17 NASB

" 'I foresaw the LORD always before my face, for He is at my right hand, that I may not be shaken. Therefore my heart rejoiced, and my tongue was glad; moreover my flesh also will rest in hope. For You will not leave my soul in Hades, nor will You allow Your Holy One to see corruption.' "
ACTS 2:25–27 NKJV

He that lives in hope dances without music.
GEORGE HERBERT

Even when there was no reason for hope, Abraham kept hoping—believing that he would become the father of many nations. For God had said to him, "That's how many descendants you will have!"
ROMANS 4:18 NLT

We boast in the hope of the glory of God. Not only so, but we also glory in our sufferings, because we know that suffering produces perseverance; perseverance, character; and character, hope. And hope does not put us to shame, because God's love has been poured out into our hearts through the Holy Spirit, who has been given to us.
ROMANS 5:2–5 NIV

And not only this, but also we ourselves, having the first fruits of the Spirit, even we ourselves groan within ourselves, waiting eagerly for our adoption as sons, the redemption of our body. For in hope we have been saved, but hope that is seen is not hope; for who hopes for what he already sees? But if we hope for what we do not see, with perseverance we wait eagerly for it.
ROMANS 8:23–25 NASB

Be joyful in hope, patient in affliction, faithful in prayer.
ROMANS 12:12 NIV

38

Hospitality

Let's face it. We're busy. Some days we just
don't have the energy to clean the house,
then entertain people. But hospitality is not
only godly—it's essential and the hallmark
of a Christ follower. Make it a point to
reach out with a cheerful heart to those
who need a delicious home-cooked meal
or a comfortable bed. Who knows? The
stranger you entertain may be an angel!

One day Elisha went to Shunem. And a well-to-do woman was there, who urged him to stay for a meal. So whenever he came by, he stopped there to eat.
2 KINGS 4:8 NIV

Hospitality should have no other nature than love.
HENRIETTA MEARS

"No sojourner had to lodge in the street, for I have opened my doors to the traveler."
JOB 31:32 NKJV

Then Melchizedek king of Salem brought out bread and wine. He was priest of God Most High.
GENESIS 14:18 NIV

*Lord, I want to serve others as You have served us—
with love, compassion, and kindness. Help me to be Your hands
and feet as I open my home to others.*

A woman named Martha opened her home to him. She had a sister called Mary, who sat at the Lord's feet listening to what he said. But Martha was distracted by all the preparations that had to be made. She came to him and asked, "Lord. . . Tell her to help me!" "Martha, Martha," the Lord answered, "you are worried and upset about many things, but few things are needed—or indeed only one. Mary has chosen what is better, and it will not be taken away from her."
LUKE 10:38–42 NIV

Who practices hospitality entertains God himself.
UNKNOWN

Share your food with the hungry and bring poor, homeless
people into your own homes. When you see someone who has
no clothes, give him yours, and don't refuse to help
your own relatives.
ISAIAH 58:7 NCV

"But when you give a reception, invite the poor, the crippled, the
lame, the blind, and you will be blessed, since they do not have
the means to repay you; for you will be repaid at the resurrection
of the righteous."
LUKE 14:13–14 NASB

There they made Him a supper; and Martha served, but Lazarus
was one of those who sat at the table with Him.
JOHN 12:2 NKJV

And when she and her household were baptized, she begged us,
saying, "If you have judged me to be faithful to the Lord,
come to my house and stay." So she persuaded us.
ACTS 16:15 NKJV

Visitor's footfalls are like medicine; they heal the sick.
AFRICAN PROVERB

Take care of God's needy people and welcome strangers
into your home.
ROMANS 12:13 CEV

And the natives showed us unusual kindness; for they kindled a
fire and made us all welcome, because of the rain that was
falling and because of the cold.
ACTS 28:2 NKJV

Eating, and hospitality in general, is a communion,
and any meal worth attending by yourself is improved
by the multiples of those with whom it is shared.
JESSE BROWNER

Overseers must be ready to welcome guests, love what is good, be wise, live right, and be holy and self-controlled.
TITUS 1:8 NCV

Do not forget to entertain strangers, for by so doing some have unwittingly entertained angels.
HEBREWS 13:2 NKJV

Use hospitality one to another without grudging.
1 PETER 4:9 KJV

It was for the sake of the Name that they went out, receiving no help from the pagans. We ought therefore to show hospitality to such people so that we may work together for the truth.
3 JOHN 1:7–8 NIV

No widow may be put on the list of widows unless she is over sixty, has been faithful to her husband, and is well known for her good deeds, such as bringing up children, showing hospitality, washing the feet of the Lord's people, helping those in trouble and devoting herself to all kinds of good deeds.
1 TIMOTHY 5:9–10 NIV

39

Infertility

The Bible has many stories of faithful, godly women who at one time were infertile or barren but went on to have children. Regardless of our fertility, our lives can be empty or full of meaning and hope. We can weep with God, like Hannah, and laugh, like Sarah. In either case, God's walking with us—through our pain and our laughter. Have hope.

If you pay attention to these laws and are careful to follow them, then the LORD your God will keep his covenant of love with you, as he swore to your ancestors. He will love you and bless you and increase your numbers. He will bless the fruit of your womb, the crops of your land—your grain, new wine and olive oil— the calves of your herds and the lambs of your flocks in the land he swore to your ancestors to give you. You will be blessed more than any other people; none of your men or women will be childless, nor will any of your livestock be without young.
DEUTERONOMY 7:12–14 NIV

> *Living in a time when the family is under attack,*
> *the real danger is idolizing the family. We hear "the family first"*
> *and may be tempted to say "amen." But Jesus will have none of this.*
> *When the family is first, God plays second fiddle.*
> WYNN KENYON

"Worship the LORD your God, and his blessing will be on your food and water. I will take away sickness from among you, and none will miscarry or be barren in your land. I will give you a full life span."
EXODUS 23:25–26 NIV

Sarai [later called Sarah] was barren; she had no children.
GENESIS 11:30 MSG

Sarah became pregnant and bore a son to Abraham in his old age, at the very time God had promised him.
GENESIS 21:2 NIV

Isaac prayed to the LORD on behalf of his wife, because she was barren; and the LORD answered him and Rebekah his wife conceived.
GENESIS 25:21 NASB

We must learn to see our circumstances through God's love,
and not God's love through our circumstances.
ANONYMOUS

When the LORD saw that Leah was unloved, he enabled her to
have children, but Rachel could not conceive.
GENESIS 29:31 NLT

Then God remembered Rachel's plight and answered her prayers
by enabling her to have children. She became pregnant and
gave birth to a son. "God has removed my disgrace," she said.
And she named him Joseph, for she said, "May the LORD add yet
another son to my family."
GENESIS 30:22–24 NLT

Now there was a certain man from Zorah, of the family of the
Danites, whose name was Manoah; and his wife was barren
and had no children. And the Angel of the LORD appeared to the
woman and said to her, "Indeed now, you are barren and have
borne no children, but you shall conceive and bear a son."
JUDGES 13:2–3 NKJV

[God] makes the barren woman abide in the house as a joyful
mother of children. Praise the LORD!
PSALM 113:9 NASB

Both of them were good people and pleased the Lord God
by obeying all that he had commanded. But they did not have
children. Elizabeth could not have any, and both Zechariah and
Elizabeth were already old.
LUKE 1:6–7 CEV

"Your relative Elizabeth is also going to have a son, even though she is old. No one thought she could ever have a baby, but in three months she will have a son. Nothing is impossible for God!"
LUKE 1:36–37 CEV

Some couples who would like to have children never do.
That does not mean God is punishing them. He may
simply have another plan for their lives.

And we know that all things work together for good to those who love God, to those who are the called according to His purpose.
ROMANS 8:28 NKJV

To know that nothing hurts the godly, is a matter of comfort; but to
be assured that all things which fall out shall cooperate for their good,
that their crosses shall be turned into blessings, that showers of affliction
water the withering root of their grace and make it flourish more;
this may fill their hearts with joy till they run over.
THOMAS WATSON

40

Joy

Joy is found in the laughter of a baby, the cuteness of a puppy, the embrace of a loved one, the warmth of a sandy beach, a just-cleaned house, an unexpected present, a meal your family raves over, an answer to prayer beyond your imagination, the quiet moments in God's presence. Embrace the joy, ladies! It's all around you. Just open your eyes—and arms!

Splendor and majesty are before him;
strength and joy are in his dwelling place.
1 Chronicles 16:27 niv

And an angel of the Lord appeared to them, and the glory of the
Lord shone around them, and they were filled with fear. And the
angel said to them, "Fear not, for behold, I bring you good news
of great joy that will be for all the people. For unto you is born
this day in the city of David a Savior, who is Christ the Lord."
Luke 2:9–11 esv

> *Be merry, really merry. The life of a true Christian should be a*
> *perpetual jubilee, a prelude to the festivals of eternity.*
> Theophane Venard

Rejoice in the Lord always: and again I say, Rejoice.
Philippians 4:4 kjv

You will show me the way of life, granting me the joy of your
presence and the pleasures of living with you forever.
Psalm 16:11 nlt

> *The out-and-out Christian is a joyful Christian. The half-and-half*
> *Christian is the kind of Christian that a great many of you are—*
> *little acquainted with the Lord. Why should we live halfway up the hill*
> *and swathed in the mists, when we might have an unclouded sky*
> *and a radiant sun over our heads if we would climb higher*
> *and walk in the light of His face?*
> Alexander MacLaren

When anxiety was great within me,
your consolation brought me joy.
Psalm 94:19 niv

The Lord is my strength and my shield; my heart trusts in him, and he helps me. My heart leaps for joy, and with my song I praise him.
PSALM 28:7 NIV

You have turned my sorrow into joyful dancing. No longer am I sad and wearing sackcloth. I thank you from my heart, and I will never stop singing your praises, my Lord and my God.
PSALM 30:11–12 CEV

Satisfy us in the morning with your unfailing love, that we may sing for joy and be glad all our days.
PSALM 90:14 NIV

> *Foolish talking and jesting are not the ways in which Christian cheerfulness should express itself, but rather "giving of thanks" (Ephesians 5:4). Religion is the source of joy and gladness, but its joy is expressed in a religious way, in thanksgiving and praise.*
> CHARLES HODGE

Worship the Lord with gladness. Come before him, singing with joy.
PSALM 100:2 NLT

A cheerful look brings joy to the heart;
good news makes for good health.
PROVERBS 15:30 NLT

"If you keep my commands, you will remain in my love, just as I have kept my Father's commands and remain in his love. I have told you this so that my joy may be in you and that your joy may be complete."
JOHN 15:10–11 NIV

"Ask [the Father], using my name, and you will receive, and you will have abundant joy."
JOHN 16:24 NLT

Joy is not necessarily the absence of suffering, it is the presence of God.
SAM STORMS

But the fruit of the Spirit is love, joy, peace, longsuffering, kindness, goodness, faithfulness.
GALATIANS 5:22 NKJV

I believe God, through His Spirit, grants us love, joy, and peace no matter what is happening in our lives. As Christians, we shouldn't expect our joy to always feel like happiness, but instead recognize joy as inner security—a safeness in our life with Christ.
JILL BRISCOE

Count it all joy, my brothers, when you meet trials of various kinds, for you know that the testing of your faith produces steadfastness.
JAMES 1:2–3 ESV

Let the sea roar, and all it contains; let the field exult, and all that is in it. Then the trees of the forest will sing for joy before the LORD; for He is coming to judge the earth. O give thanks to the LORD, for He is good; for His lovingkindness is everlasting.
1 CHRONICLES 16:32–34 NASB

The hope of the righteous brings joy, but the expectation of the wicked will perish.
PROVERBS 10:28 ESV

41

Loneliness

There are times when, due to life circumstances, we are alone. Perhaps a husband has died, a child has moved away, or a friend has rejected us. Even in a crowd we may feel moments of loneliness. But in reality, we are never alone. God is here. Pray. Reach out to Jesus, pull Him to your side. Then, forgetting self, reach out to others. You weren't meant to go it alone.

Loneliness is the first thing which God's eye named, not good.
JOHN MILTON

Then the LORD God said, "It is not good for the man to be alone.
I will make a helper who is just right for him."
GENESIS 2:18 NLT

"You and these people who come to you will only wear yourselves
out. The work is too heavy for you; you cannot handle it alone."
EXODUS 18:18 NIV

*God, hold me in Your arms. With You in my life, I am never really
alone. Remain here beside me as I reach out in love to others.*

Even when I walk through the darkest valley, I will not be afraid,
for you are close beside me. Your rod and your staff
protect and comfort me.
PSALM 23:4 NLT

Turn to me and have mercy on me, because I am lonely and hurting.
PSALM 25:16 NCV

*Language. . .has created the word "loneliness"
to express the pain of being alone. And it has created the
word "solitude" to express the glory of being alone.*
PAUL TILLICH

God places the solitary in families and gives the desolate
a home in which to dwell.
PSALM 68:6 AMP

I lie awake, I have become like a lonely bird on a housetop.
PSALM 102:7 NASB

Again, if two lie down together, they will keep warm;
but how can one be warm alone?
ECCLESIASTES 4:11 NKJV

When we truly realize that we are all alone
is when we need others the most.
RONALD ANTHONY

" 'Fear not, for I am with you; be not dismayed, for I am your
God. I will strengthen you, yes, I will help you, I will uphold you
with My righteous right hand.' "
ISAIAH 41:10 NKJV

Jesus could no longer openly enter the city, but was outside in
deserted places; and they came to Him from every direction.
MARK 1:45 NKJV

"The one who sent me is with me. I always do what pleases him,
and he will never leave me."
JOHN 8:29 CEV

The time will come and is already here when all of you will
be scattered. Each of you will go back home and leave me by
myself. But the Father will be with me, and I won't be alone.
JOHN 16:32 CEV

For none of us lives for ourselves alone, and none of us dies
for ourselves alone.
ROMANS 14:7 NIV

Be satisfied with what you have. For God has said, "I will never
fail you. I will never abandon you."
HEBREWS 13:5 NLT

Loneliness accepted becomes a gift leading one from a life dominated by tears to the discovery of one's true self and finally to the heart of longing and the love of God.
UNKNOWN

Since we want to become spiritually one with the Master, we must not pursue the kind of sex that avoids commitment and intimacy, leaving us more lonely than ever—the kind of sex that can never "become one."
1 CORINTHIANS 6:17 MSG

Now a true widow, a woman who is truly alone in this world, has placed her hope in God. She prays night and day, asking God for his help.
1 TIMOTHY 5:5 NLT

42
Loving Others

It may be difficult to be keen on others, especially when they have wronged us. But God wants us to love everyone—in all situations! In doing so, we free ourselves from the poison of bitterness, grudges, and unforgiveness. So no matter what your husband, daughter, son, mother, father, sibling, friend, or enemy has done, love them. And let freedom ring!

"A new command I give you: Love one another. As I have loved you, so you must love one another. By this everyone will know that you are my disciples, if you love one another."
JOHN 13:34–35 NIV

This is how we know what love is: Jesus Christ laid down his life for us. And we ought to lay down our lives for our brothers and sisters.
1 JOHN 3:16 NIV

My dear, dear friends, if God loved us like this, we certainly ought to love each other. No one has seen God, ever. But if we love one another, God dwells deeply within us, and his love becomes complete in us—perfect love!
1 JOHN 4:11–12 MSG

If I belittle those whom I am called to serve, talk of their weak points in contrast perhaps with what I think of as my strong points; if I adopt a superior attitude. . .then I know nothing of Calvary love.
AMY CARMICHAEL

And this is his command: to believe in the name of his Son, Jesus Christ, and to love one another as he commanded us.
1 JOHN 3:23 NIV

The one who loves his brother abides in the Light and there is no cause for stumbling in him.
1 JOHN 2:10 NASB

I want the love that cannot help but love; loving, like God, for very sake of love.
A. B. SIMPSON

Love each other with genuine affection, and take delight in honoring each other.
ROMANS 12:10 NLT

Finally, all of you should be of one mind. Sympathize with each other. Love each other as brothers and sisters. Be tenderhearted, and keep a humble attitude.
1 PETER 3:8 NLT

When anger wins, love always loses.
WILLARD HARLEY JR.

Be completely humble and gentle; be patient, bearing with one another in love. Make every effort to keep the unity of the Spirit through the bond of peace.
EPHESIANS 4:2–3 NIV

For you have been called to live in freedom, my brothers and sisters. But don't use your freedom to satisfy your sinful nature. Instead, use your freedom to serve one another in love.
GALATIANS 5:13 NLT

Owe no one anything, except to love each other, for the one who loves another has fulfilled the law. For the commandments, "You shall not commit adultery, You shall not murder, You shall not steal, You shall not covet," and any other commandment, are summed up in this word: "You shall love your neighbor as yourself."
ROMANS 13:8–9 ESV

Love is an act of endless forgiveness.
JEAN VANIER

And let us consider how to stir up one another to love and good
works, not neglecting to meet together, as is the habit of some,
but encouraging one another, and all the more as you see
the Day drawing near.
HEBREWS 10:24–25 ESV

Beloved, let us love one another, for love is from God;
and everyone who loves is born of God and knows God.
The one who does not love does not know God, for God is love.
1 JOHN 4:7–8 NASB

Make every effort to add to your faith goodness; and to
goodness, knowledge; and to knowledge, self-control; and to
self-control, perseverance; and to perseverance, godliness;
and to godliness, mutual affection; and to mutual affection, love.
2 PETER 1:5–7 NIV

But if anyone has the world's goods and sees his brother in
need, yet closes his heart against him, how does God's love
abide in him?
1 JOHN 3:17 ESV

43
Marriage

Once you say, "I do," you and your husband
become one. Together you meet the challenges of
the world—child rearing, employment, finances,
home ownership, and so on. As the years pass, you
will have numerous ups and downs. But you will
reap a wonderful harvest if you stick with your
man, through thick and thin, and tend your union
like a garden—watering it with love, affection,
and attention. Ah, it's Eden all over again!

The LORD God said, "It isn't good for the man to live alone.
I need to make a suitable partner for him."
GENESIS 2:18 CEV

"But when God made the world, 'he made them male and female.
So a man will leave his father and mother and be united with
his wife, and the two will become one body.' So there are not
two, but one. God has joined the two together, so no one should
separate them."
MARK 10:6–9 NCV

Love isn't selfish or quick tempered. It doesn't keep a record of
wrongs that others do.
1 CORINTHIANS 13:5 CEV

> *If love does not know how to give and take without restrictions,*
> *it is not love, but a transaction that never fails to lay stress*
> *on a plus and a minus.*
> EMMA GOLDMAN

Submit to one another out of reverence for Christ.
EPHESIANS 5:21 NIV

Each one of you must love his wife as he loves himself,
and a wife must respect her husband.
EPHESIANS 5:33 NCV

Marriage should be honored by everyone, and husband and wife
should keep their marriage pure. God will judge as guilty those
who take part in sexual sins.
HEBREWS 13:4 NCV

We must not just please ourselves. We should help others do
what is right and build them up in the Lord.
ROMANS 15:1–2 NLT

Marriage is like panty hose; it all depends on what you put into it.
PHYLLIS SCHLAFLY

May the God who gives endurance and encouragement give you
the same attitude of mind toward each other that Christ Jesus
had, so that with one mind and one voice you may glorify the
God and Father of our Lord Jesus Christ. Accept one another,
then, just as Christ accepted you, in order to bring praise to God.
ROMANS 15:5–7 NIV

The husband should fulfill his wife's sexual needs,
and the wife should fulfill her husband's needs.
1 CORINTHIANS 7:3 NLT

Her husband can trust her, and she will greatly enrich his life.
She brings him good, not harm, all the days of her life.
PROVERBS 31:11–12 NLT

Husbands are like fires, they go out when unattended.
ZSA ZSA GABOR

For the unbelieving husband is sanctified by the wife, and the
unbelieving wife is sanctified by the husband; otherwise your
children would be unclean, but now they are holy.
1 CORINTHIANS 7:14 NKJV

Don't you wives realize that your husbands might be saved because of you? And don't you husbands realize that your wives might be saved because of you?

1 CORINTHIANS 7:16 NLT

"Where you go I will go, and where you lodge I will lodge. Your people shall be my people, and your God my God. Where you die I will die, and there will I be buried. May the LORD do so to me and more also if anything but death parts me from you."

RUTH 1:16–17 ESV

Marriage is like a three-speed gearbox: affection, friendship, love.
PETER USTINOV

She is clothed with strength and dignity;
she can laugh at the days to come.

PROVERBS 31:25 NIV

Lord, thank You for my husband. Help me to love him as You love me—unconditionally and completely!

Her children praise her, and with great pride her husband says, "There are many good women, but you are the best!"

PROVERBS 31:28–29 CEV

44

Ministry

God calls women to love Him and to love
others as ourselves. That means serving God
and others in whatever way He has gifted us—
mentoring younger women, teaching children,
leading worship, serving on a missions trip, or
some other service. A new ministry may mean
leaving your comfort zone for a "God zone," but
who knows? You may be another Deborah—
a prophet, wife, leader, and judge! Her husband
can trust her, and she will greatly enrich his life.

We have different gifts, according to the grace given to each of us. If your gift is prophesying, then prophesy in accordance with your faith; if it is serving, then serve; if it is teaching, then teach; if it is to encourage, then give encouragement; if it is giving, then give generously; if it is to lead, do it diligently; if it is to show mercy, do it cheerfully.
ROMANS 12:6–8 NIV

As each one has received a gift, minister it to one another, as good stewards of the manifold grace of God. . . . If anyone ministers, let him do it as with the ability which God supplies, that in all things God may be glorified through Jesus Christ.
1 PETER 4:10–11 NKJV

We've been called, and He has blessed.
WILLIE AAMES

You, my brothers and sisters, were called to be free. But do not use your freedom to indulge the flesh; rather, serve one another humbly in love.
GALATIANS 5:13 NIV

"Who knows whether you have not come to the kingdom for such a time as this?"
ESTHER 4:14 ESV

Now Deborah, a prophet, the wife of Lappidoth, was leading Israel at that time. She held court under the Palm of Deborah. . . and the Israelites went up to her to have their disputes decided.
JUDGES 4:4–5 NIV

What do we live for, if not to make life less difficult for each other?
GEORGE ELIOT

Then Miriam the prophet, Aaron's sister, took a tambourine and led all the women as they played their tambourines and danced.
Exodus 15:20 NLT

There was also a prophet, Anna. . . . She never left the temple but worshiped night and day, fasting and praying.
Luke 2:36–37 NIV

In the city of Joppa there was a follower named Tabitha (whose Greek name was Dorcas). She was always doing good deeds and kind acts.
Acts 9:36 NCV

The human contribution is the essential ingredient.
It is only in the giving of oneself to others that we truly live.
Ethel Percy Andrus

Philip the Evangelist. . .had four unmarried daughters who had the gift of prophecy.
Acts 21:8–9 NLT

"See to it that you complete the ministry you have received in the Lord."
Colossians 4:17 NIV

Teach older women to be holy in their behavior, not speaking against others or enslaved to too much wine, but teaching what is good. Then they can teach the young women to love their husbands, to love their children, to be wise and pure, to be good workers at home, to be kind, and to yield to their husbands.
Titus 2:3–5 NCV

45

Money

The Bible is full of advice on how to view and handle money. One oft-repeated tenet is to not hoard but use our coin to help others—not only because the more we give, the more we get, but because that's what God wants us to do. Used wisely, money won't become a bone of contention between husbands and wives and will prevent singletons from drowning in debt.

A hard worker has plenty of food, but a person who chases fantasies ends up in poverty.
PROVERBS 28:19 NLT

Dishonest money dwindles away, but whoever gathers money little by little makes it grow.
PROVERBS 13:11 NIV

Money will come when you are doing the right thing.
MIKE PHILLIPS

"For which one of you, when he wants to build a tower, does not first sit down and calculate the cost to see if he has enough to complete it? Otherwise, when he has laid a foundation and is not able to finish, all who observe it begin to ridicule him."
LUKE 14:28–29 NASB

The wise have wealth and luxury, but fools spend whatever they get.
PROVERBS 21:20 NLT

Just as the rich rule the poor, so the borrower is servant to the lender.
PROVERBS 22:7 NLT

Owe no one anything except to love one another, for he who loves another has fulfilled the law.
ROMANS 13:8 NKJV

"No one can serve two masters. The person will hate one master and love the other, or will follow one master and refuse to follow the other. You cannot serve both God and worldly riches."
MATTHEW 6:24 NCV

If you want to see what God thinks of money,
just look at all the people He gave it to.
DOROTHY PARKER

Give me an eagerness for your laws rather than a love for money!
PSALM 119:36 NLT

Lust for money brings trouble and nothing but trouble.
1 TIMOTHY 6:10 MSG

If you love money and wealth, you will never be satisfied
with what you have.
ECCLESIASTES 5:10 CEV

Money never made a man happy yet, nor will it. The more a man has,
the more he wants. Instead of filling a vacuum, it makes one.
BENJAMIN FRANKLIN

Keep your lives free from the love of money
and be content with what you have.
HEBREWS 13:5 NIV

"For what will it profit a man if he gains the whole world,
and loses his own soul?"
MARK 8:36 NKJV

Money often costs too much.
RALPH WALDO EMERSON

On the first day of every week, each one of you should set aside
a sum of money in keeping with your income, saving it up,
so that when I come no collections will have to be made.
1 CORINTHIANS 16:2 NIV

"Give, and it will be given to you: good measure, pressed down, shaken together, and running over will be put into your bosom. For with the same measure that you use, it will be measured back to you."
LUKE 6:38 NKJV

You have not lived a perfect day, even though you have earned your money, unless you have done something for someone who will never be able to repay you.
RUTH SMELTZER

He said to them, Pay therefore to Caesar the things that are due to Caesar, and pay to God the things that are due to God.
MATTHEW 22:21 AMP

And my God shall supply all your need according to His riches in glory by Christ Jesus.
PHILIPPIANS 4:19 NKJV

"Bring all the tithes into the storehouse so there will be enough food in my Temple. If you do," says the LORD of Heaven's Armies, "I will open the windows of heaven for you. I will pour out a blessing so great you won't have enough room to take it in! Try it! Put me to the test!"
MALACHI 3:10 NLT

Honor the LORD with your wealth and with the best part of everything you produce. Then he will fill your barns with grain, and your vats will overflow with good wine.
PROVERBS 3:9–10 NLT

46

Patience

In this hectic day and age, it's easy for moms
to lose patience with children who disregard
"house rules," husbands who ignore pleas to fix
the leaky faucet, bosses who seem oblivious to
our hard work, friends who never return calls,
a God who's slow in answering prayer. But we
are to be as patient with others as the Lord is
with us. Now that's a virtue to strive for!

Then he passed in front of Moses and called out, "I am the LORD God. I am merciful and very patient with my people. I show great love, and I can be trusted."
EXODUS 34:6 CEV

The LORD is merciful! He is kind and patient,
and his love never fails.
PSALM 103:8 CEV

> *Patience with others is love, patience with self is hope,*
> *patience with God is faith.*
> ADEL BESTAVROS

Do you think lightly of the riches of His kindness and tolerance and patience, not knowing that the kindness of God leads you to repentance?
ROMANS 2:4 NASB

Wait patiently for the LORD. Be brave and courageous.
Yes, wait patiently for the LORD.
PSALM 27:14 NLT

Better to be patient than powerful;
better to have self-control than to conquer a city.
PROVERBS 16:32 NLT

Be still before the LORD and wait patiently for him; do not fret when people succeed in their ways, when they carry out their wicked schemes.
PSALM 37:7 NIV

Teach the older men to exercise self-control, to be worthy of respect, and to live wisely. They must have sound faith and be filled with love and patience.
Titus 2:2 NLT

Teach us, O Lord, the disciplines of patience,
for to wait is often harder than to work.
Peter Marshall

Rejoice in our confident hope.
Be patient in trouble, and keep on praying.
Romans 12:12 NLT

For whatever things were written before were written for our learning, that we through the patience and comfort of the Scriptures might have hope.
Romans 15:4 NKJV

Patience is a grace as difficult as it is necessary,
and as hard to come by as it is precious when it is gained.
C. H. Spurgeon

We work wearily with our own hands to earn our living. We bless those who curse us. We are patient with those who abuse us.
1 Corinthians 4:12 NLT

Love is patient, love is kind and is not jealous;
love does not brag and is not arrogant.
1 Corinthians 13:4 NASB

Be completely humble and gentle;
be patient, bearing with one another in love.
Ephesians 4:2 NIV

Brothers and sisters, we urge you to warn those who are lazy. Encourage those who are timid. Take tender care of those who are weak. Be patient with everyone.

1 THESSALONIANS 5:14 NLT

Biblically, waiting is not just something we have to do until we get what we want. Waiting is part of the process of becoming what God wants us to be.

JOHN ORTBERG

I pray that the Lord will guide you to be as loving as God and as patient as Christ.

2 THESSALONIANS 3:5 CEV

The Lord's bond-servant must not be quarrelsome, but be kind to all, able to teach, patient when wronged.

2 TIMOTHY 2:24 NASB

For God is pleased with you when you do what you know is right and patiently endure unfair treatment. Of course, you get no credit for being patient if you are beaten for doing wrong. But if you suffer for doing good and endure it patiently, God is pleased with you.

1 PETER 2:19–20 NLT

Through patience a ruler can be persuaded, and a gentle tongue can break a bone.

PROVERBS 25:15 NIV

The principal part of faith is patience.

GEORGE MACDONALD

God's Spirit makes us loving, happy, peaceful,
patient, kind, good, faithful.
GALATIANS 5:22 CEV

Therefore, as God's chosen people, holy and dearly loved,
clothe yourselves with compassion, kindness, humility,
gentleness and patience.
COLOSSIANS 3:12 NIV

Endeavor to be always patient of the faults and imperfections of others,
for thou hast many faults and imperfections of thy own
that require a reciprocation of forbearance.
THOMAS À KEMPIS

And the Scriptures give us hope and encouragement as we wait
patiently for God's promises to be fulfilled. May God, who gives
this patience and encouragement, help you live in complete
harmony with each other, as is fitting for followers of Christ Jesus.
ROMANS 15:4–5 NLT

47

Peace

The peace of this world is elusive, at best.
Our only hope is the peace we find when
we walk closely with Jesus. This serenity,
beyond all understanding, is something we
need to connect with every day. Find some
space to be alone, to be still, to be at peace
through Christ. Ladies, it's essential to life.

Therefore, since we have been justified by faith, we have peace with God through our Lord Jesus Christ.
ROMANS 5:1 ESV

My Soul, there is a country
Far beyond the stars,
Where stands a winged sentry
All skillful in the wars;
There, above noise and danger
Sweet peace sits, crown'd with smiles,
And One born in a manger
Commands the beauteous files.
HENRY VAUGHAN

For to us a child is born, to us a son is given, and the government will be on his shoulders. And he will be called Wonderful Counselor, Mighty God, Everlasting Father, Prince of Peace. Of the greatness of his government and peace there will be no end. He will reign on David's throne and over his kingdom, establishing and upholding it with justice and righteousness from that time on and forever.
ISAIAH 9:6–7 NIV

Peace with God does not always mean a calm time of happiness.
The salvation that Jesus brought comes with a price:
conflict against evil. But, in the end, all who trust in Him
experience the peace of eternal life.

"But whoever denies Me before men, I will also deny him before My Father who is in heaven. Do not think that I came to bring peace on the earth; I did not come to bring peace, but a sword."
MATTHEW 10:33–34 NASB

" 'The LORD bless you, and keep you; the LORD make His face shine on you, and be gracious to you; the LORD lift up His countenance on you, and give you peace.' "
NUMBERS 6:24–26 NASB

For the mind set on the flesh is death, but the mind set on the Spirit is life and peace.
ROMANS 8:6 NASB

> *God cannot give us happiness and peace apart from Himself, because it is not there. There is no such thing.*
> C. S. LEWIS

Depart from evil and do good; seek peace and pursue it.
PSALM 34:14 NASB

"The LORD gives perfect peace to those whose faith is firm."
ISAIAH 26:3 CEV

> *Peacemakers carry about with them an atmosphere in which quarrels die a natural death.*
> R. T. ARCHIBALD

"Peace I leave with you, My peace I give to you; not as the world gives do I give to you. Let not your heart be troubled, neither let it be afraid."
JOHN 14:27 NKJV

If it is possible, as far as it depends on you, live at peace with everyone.
ROMANS 12:18 NIV

Finally, brothers, rejoice. Aim for restoration, comfort one another, agree with one another, live in peace; and the God of love and peace will be with you.
2 Corinthians 13:11 esv

And let the peace that comes from Christ rule in your hearts. For as members of one body you are called to live in peace. And always be thankful.
Colossians 3:15 nlt

And therefore you who think so basely of the Gospel and the professors of it, because at present their peace and comfort are not come, should know that it is on the way to them, and comes to stay everlastingly with them; whereas your peace is going from you every moment, and is sure to leave you without any hope of returning to you again. Look not how the Christian begins, but ends.
William Gurnall

"There is no peace for the wicked," says the Lord.
Isaiah 48:22 nasb

Those who love Your law have great peace,
and nothing causes them to stumble.
Psalm 119:165 nasb

Mark the blameless man, and observe the upright;
for the future of that man is peace.
Psalm 37:37 nkjv

Peace is always beautiful.
Walt Whitman

48

Perseverance

If you keep your eyes on Jesus, you can endure
anything. No matter how weary or discouraged
you become, God will help you keep on
keeping on. That's His promise, woman!
God knows what you're going through. So
never give up! Never surrender! For myriad
rewards await the persistent woman!

Now it came about, as she continued praying before the LORD, that Eli was watching her mouth. . . . It came about in due time, after Hannah had conceived, that she gave birth to a son; and she named him Samuel, saying, "Because I have asked him of the LORD."
1 SAMUEL 1:12, 20 NASB

Persist and persevere, and you will find
most things that are attainable, possible.
LORD CHESTERFIELD

[King Uzziah] continued to seek God in the days of Zechariah, who had understanding through the vision of God; and as long as he sought the LORD, God prospered him.
2 CHRONICLES 26:5 NASB

Our enemies were trying to frighten us and to keep us from our work. But I asked God to give me strength. . . . When our enemies in the surrounding nations learned that the work was finished, they felt helpless, because they knew that our God had helped us rebuild the wall.
NEHEMIAH 6:9, 16 CEV

The will to persevere is often the difference between failure and success.
DAVID SARNOFF

There was a widow who kept going to the judge and saying, "Make sure that I get fair treatment in court." For a while the judge refused to do anything. Finally, he said to himself, "Even though I don't fear God or care about people, I will help this widow because she keeps on bothering me. If I don't help her, she will wear me out."
LUKE 18:3–5 CEV

Keep on asking and it will be given you; keep on seeking and you will find; keep on knocking [reverently] and [the door] will be opened to you.

MATTHEW 7:7 AMP

Perseverance is a great element of success. If you only knock long enough and loud enough at the gate, you are sure to wake up somebody.

HENRY WADSWORTH LONGFELLOW

For if we are faithful to the end, trusting God just as firmly as when we first believed, we will share in all that belongs to Christ.

HEBREWS 3:14 NLT

The rewards for those who persevere far exceed the pain that must precede the victory.

TED W. ENGSTROM

Now finish the work, so that your eager willingness to do it may be matched by your completion of it, according to your means.

2 CORINTHIANS 8:11 NIV

And I am certain that God, who began the good work within you, will continue his work until it is finally finished on the day when Christ Jesus returns.

PHILIPPIANS 1:6 NLT

We also glory in our sufferings, because we know that suffering produces perseverance; perseverance, character; and character, hope.

ROMANS 5:3–4 NIV

God, please give me the confidence to continue in my endeavors. Fill me with the energy I need to do the next thing.

We have confidence in the Lord that you are doing and will
continue to do the things we command. May the Lord direct your
hearts into God's love and Christ's perseverance.
2 Thessalonians 3:4–5 niv

And let us run with endurance the race God has set before us.
We do this by keeping our eyes on Jesus, the champion who
initiates and perfects our faith.
Hebrews 12:1–2 nlt

Dear brothers and sisters, when troubles come your way,
consider it an opportunity for great joy. For you know that when
your faith is tested, your endurance has a chance to grow. So let
it grow, for when your endurance is fully developed, you will be
perfect and complete, needing nothing.
James 1:2–4 nlt

We count as blessed those who have persevered. You have
heard of Job's perseverance and have seen what the Lord finally
brought about. The Lord is full of compassion and mercy.
James 5:11 niv

Perseverance is failing nineteen times and succeeding the twentieth.
Julie Andrews

Make every effort to add to your faith goodness; and to
goodness, knowledge; and to knowledge, self-control; and to
self-control, perseverance; and to perseverance, godliness;
and to godliness, mutual affection; and to mutual affection, love.
2 Peter 1:5–7 niv

"'I know your deeds, and your love and faith and service and perseverance, and that your deeds of late are greater than at first.'"
REVELATION 2:19 NASB

> *By perseverance the snail reached the ark.*
> C. H. SPURGEON

"All who are victorious will inherit all these blessings, and I will be their God, and they will be my children."
REVELATION 21:7 NLT

> *I think that if my kids are completely convinced of God's unfailing love for them, whether they fail or not, they'll have confidence to persevere in life.*
> AMY GRANT

49

Physical Appearance

Let's admit it, ladies. Most times we tend
to judge other women (and men) by their
appearance. But that's not what the Lord would
have us do. Instead, we must look beneath
the surface and ask God to show us the heart
of people. And, while we're at it, let's take a
good look at ourselves. Are we spending more
time on the inner than the outer woman?

"The LORD does not look at the things people look at. People look at the outward appearance, but the LORD looks at the heart."
1 SAMUEL 16:7 NIV

I have never known a really chic woman whose appearance was not, in large part, an outward reflection of her inner self.
MAINBOCHER

Wisdom lights up a person's face, softening its harshness.
ECCLESIASTES 8:1 NLT

Don't judge by appearances. Judge by what is right.
JOHN 7:24 CEV

Charm is deceitful and beauty is vain, but a woman who fears the LORD, she shall be praised.
PROVERBS 31:30 NASB

"'But you trusted in your beauty and used your fame to become a prostitute. You lavished your favors on anyone who passed by and your beauty became his.'"
EZEKIEL 16:15 NIV

"Your heart was lifted up because of your beauty;
you corrupted your wisdom for the sake of your splendor."
EZEKIEL 28:17 NKJV

Fashion is the science of appearance, and it inspires one with the desire to seem rather than to be.
HENRY FIELDING

Your beauty should not come from outward adornment, such as elaborate hairstyles and the wearing of gold jewelry or fine clothes. Rather, it should be that of your inner self, the unfading beauty of a gentle and quiet spirit, which is of great worth in God's sight. For this is the way the holy women of the past who put their hope in God used to adorn themselves.

1 PETER 3:3–5 NIV

And I want women to get in there with the men in humility before God, not primping before a mirror or chasing the latest fashions but doing something beautiful for God and becoming beautiful doing it.

1 TIMOTHY 2:9–10 MSG

Let us be grateful to the mirror for revealing to us our appearance only.

SAMUEL BUTLER

"Just as you can identify a tree by its fruit, so you can identify people by their actions."

MATTHEW 7:20 NLT

Attitude is more important than the past, than education, than money, than circumstances, than what people do or say. It is more important than appearance, giftedness, or skill.

CHARLES R. SWINDOLL

Don't copy the behavior and customs of this world, but let God transform you into a new person by changing the way you think. Then you will learn to know God's will for you, which is good and pleasing and perfect.

ROMANS 12:2 NLT

We should look to the mind, and not to the outward appearance.

AESOP

50

Plans

When our plans are going awry, it's time to
stop and consider: who's at the helm—
us or God? Perhaps it's time to sail back
into the harbor of God's Word and get some
new direction from the Lord. Then, and only
then, will it be safe to set back out into the
sea of life, sure we're on the right course.

*Our plans miscarry because they have no aim. When a man does not
know what harbor he is making for, no wind is the right wind.*
                                        LUCIUS ANNAEUS SENECA

"But when he, the Spirit of truth, comes, he will guide you into all
the truth. He will not speak on his own; he will speak only what
he hears, and he will tell you what is yet to come."
JOHN 16:13 NIV

Your ears shall hear a word behind you, saying, "This is the way,
walk in it," whenever you turn to the right hand or whenever you
turn to the left.
ISAIAH 30:21 NKJV

*Abba God, I don't know which way to turn. Be my guide, show me
which way to go. I want to walk in Your will, not mine.*

You guide me with your counsel,
and afterward you will take me into glory.
PSALM 73:24 NIV

I should be making plans more for the next world than for this one.
                                        GIULIO ANDREOTTI

"The LORD will guide you always; he will satisfy your needs in a
sun-scorched land and will strengthen your frame. You will be like
a well-watered garden, like a spring whose waters never fail."
ISAIAH 58:11 NIV

Many are the plans in a person's heart,
but it is the LORD's purpose that prevails.
PROVERBS 19:21 NIV

I find that doing of the will of God leaves me no time
for disputing about His plans.
GEORGE MACDONALD

"I had it in my heart to build a house as a place of rest for the ark of the covenant of the LORD, for the footstool of our God, and I made plans to build it. But God said to me, 'You are not to build a house for my Name, because you are a warrior and have shed blood.' "
1 CHRONICLES 28:2–3 NIV

When defeat comes, accept it as a signal that your plans are not sound,
rebuild those plans, and set sail once more toward your coveted goal.
NAPOLEON HILL

He gave him the plans of all that the Spirit had put in his mind for the courts of the temple of the LORD.
1 CHRONICLES 28:12 NIV

Plans are only good intentions unless they immediately
degenerate into hard work.
PETER DRUCKER

Then they believed his promises and sang his praise. But they soon forgot what he had done and did not wait for his plan to unfold.
PSALM 106:12–13 NIV

If you plan to do evil, you will be lost; if you plan to do good, you will receive unfailing love and faithfulness.
PROVERBS 14:22 NLT

The plans of the LORD stand firm forever, the purposes of his heart through all generations.
PSALM 33:11 NIV

If you want to make God laugh, tell Him about your plans.
WOODY ALLEN

What you ought to say is, "If the Lord wants us to, we will live and do this or that." Otherwise you are boasting about your own plans, and all such boasting is evil.
JAMES 4:15–16 NLT

Commit to the LORD whatever you do,
and he will establish your plans.
PROVERBS 16:3 NIV

Speak to Him often of your business, your plans, your troubles,
your fears—of everything that concerns you.
ALPHONSUS LIGUORI

For You are my rock and my fortress; for Your name's sake
You will lead me and guide me.
PSALM 31:3 NASB

" 'For I know the plans that I have for you,' declares the LORD,
'plans for welfare and not for calamity to give you a future
and a hope.' "
JEREMIAH 29:11 NASB

May he grant your heart's desires and make
all your plans succeed.
PSALM 20:4 NLT

It's fascinating for us women to begin looking at our lives in five-year
plans. It really does help you keep on track. If that's too hard,
start with a two-year plan.
MARLO THOMAS

51

Possessions

Possessions aren't bad, per se. After all, we're
God's precious possession (yes, precious!).
The trouble arises when we fear losing what
we have already gained or are possessed by our
possessions. God wants us to live simply, treat
our possessions as gifts from Him, and store our
treasures in heaven. Instead of hoarding (do we
really need all those shoes?), share with those less
fortunate. In doing so, you will be free indeed!

*Lord, thank You for blessing me with more than I need. Give me
direction as to what and how much to share with others.
And I'll give You the glory! Amen!*

For you are a people holy to the Lord your God. The Lord your
God has chosen you out of all the peoples on the face of the
earth to be his people, his treasured possession.
Deuteronomy 7:6 niv

You are royal priests, a holy nation, God's very own possession.
As a result, you can show others the goodness of God, for he
called you out of the darkness into his wonderful light.
1 Peter 2:9 nlt

Treasure your relationships, not your possessions.
Anthony J. D'Angelo

"The Lord will command the blessing upon you in your barns and
in all that you put your hand to, and He will bless you in the land
which the Lord your God gives you."
Deuteronomy 28:8 nasb

Of all our possessions, wisdom alone is immortal.
Isocrates

Then Jesus, looking at him, loved him, and said to him, "One
thing you lack: Go your way, sell whatever you have and give to
the poor, and you will have treasure in heaven; and come, take
up the cross, and follow Me." But he was sad at this word,
and went away sorrowful, for he had great possessions.
Mark 10:21–22 nkjv

Turn my heart toward your statutes and not toward selfish gain.
PSALM 119:36 NIV

Anything you cannot relinquish when it has outlived its usefulness possesses you, and in this materialistic age a great many of us are possessed by our possessions.
PEACE PILGRIM

Naked (without possessions) came I [into this world] from my mother's womb, and naked (without possessions) shall I depart. The Lord gave and the Lord has taken away; blessed (praised and magnified in worship) be the name of the Lord!
JOB 1:21 AMP

Do not be overawed when others grow rich, when the splendor of their houses increases; for they will take nothing with them when they die, their splendor will not descend with them.
PSALM 49:16–17 NIV

Wealth consists not in having great possessions, but in having few wants.
EPICTETUS

Serving God does make us very rich, if we are satisfied with what we have. We brought nothing into the world, so we can take nothing out.
1 TIMOTHY 6:6–7 NCV

As servants of God we commend ourselves in every way. . . poor, yet making many rich; having nothing, and yet possessing everything.
2 CORINTHIANS 6:4, 10 NIV

All the Lord's followers often met together, and they shared everything they had. They would sell their property and possessions and give the money to whoever needed it. . . . They broke bread together in different homes and shared their food happily and freely, while praising God.
ACTS 2:44–47 CEV

And though I bestow all my goods to feed the poor, and though I give my body to be burned, but have not love, it profits me nothing.
1 CORINTHIANS 13:3 NKJV

> *Material possessions, winning scores, and great reputations are meaningless in the eyes of the Lord, because He knows what we really are and that is all that matters.*
> JOHN WOODEN

But whoever has this world's goods, and sees his brother in need, and shuts up his heart from him, how does the love of God abide in him?
1 JOHN 3:17 NKJV

Then He [Jesus] said to them, "Beware, and be on your guard against every form of greed; for not even when one has an abundance does his life consist of his possessions."
LUKE 12:15 NASB

> *To attain inner peace you must actually give your life, not just your possessions. When you at last give your life—bringing into alignment your beliefs and the way you live then, and only then, can you begin to find inner peace.*
> PEACE PILGRIM

What will you gain, if you own the whole world but destroy yourself? What would you give to get back your soul?

Matthew 16:26 cev

A free life cannot acquire many possessions, because this is not easy to do without servility to mobs or monarchs.

Epicurus

"Do not worry about your life, as to what you will eat; nor for your body, as to what you will put on. For life is more than food, and the body more than clothing."

Luke 12:22–23 nasb

"The seeds that fell among the thorns represent those who hear the message, but all too quickly the message is crowded out by the cares and riches and pleasures of this life. And so they never grow into maturity."

Luke 8:14 nlt

I consider everything a loss because of the surpassing worth of knowing Christ Jesus my Lord, for whose sake I have lost all things. I consider them garbage, that I may gain Christ.

Philippians 3:8 niv

52

Prayer

God wants to know everything that's on your
mind, every burden you carry. It's not that
He doesn't know what you're going through.
It's just that He wants you to come to Him
in prayer. Even if you can't find the words,
come—anywhere, anytime, anyplace. God
will lift your burdens and give the newly
unencumbered you the power to move mountains.
Muscle up, woman! It's prayer time!

The LORD detests the sacrifice of the wicked, but he delights in the prayers of the upright.
PROVERBS 15:8 NLT

He will respond to the prayer of the destitute;
he will not despise their plea.
PSALM 102:17 NIV

Do not be anxious about anything, but in every situation, by prayer and petition, with thanksgiving, present your requests to God.
PHILIPPIANS 4:6 NIV

Never wait for fitter time or place to talk to Him. To wait till you go to church or to your closet is to make Him wait. He will listen as you walk.
GEORGE MACDONALD

Pray in the Spirit at all times and on every occasion. Stay alert and be persistent in your prayers for all believers everywhere.
EPHESIANS 6:18 NLT

Pray without ceasing.
1 THESSALONIANS 5:17 KJV

We are too busy to pray, and so we are too busy to have power. We have a great deal of activity, but we accomplish little; many services but few conversions; much machinery but few results.
R. A. TORREY

I want everyone everywhere to lift innocent hands toward heaven and pray, without being angry or arguing with each other.
1 TIMOTHY 2:8 CEV

The spirit of prayer is a pressing forth of the soul out of this earthly life, it is a stretching with all its desire after the life of God, it is a leaving, as far as it can, all its own spirit, to receive a spirit from above, to be one life, one love, one spirit with Christ in God.
WILLIAM LAW

Answer me when I call to you, my righteous God. Give me relief from my distress; have mercy on me and hear my prayer.
PSALM 4:1 NIV

The LORD has heard my plea; the LORD accepts my prayer.
PSALM 6:9 ESV

We worship you, Lord, and we should always pray whenever we find out that we have sinned. Then we won't be swept away by a raging flood.
PSALM 32:6 CEV

If God can bring blessing from the broken body of Jesus and glory from something that's as obscene as the cross, He can bring blessing from my problems and my pain and my unanswered prayer. I just have to trust Him.
ANNE GRAHAM LOTZ

I am the one who has seen the afflictions that come from the rod of the LORD's anger. . . . He has walled me in, and I cannot escape. He has bound me in heavy chains. And though I cry and shout, he has shut out my prayers. . . . Yet I still dare to hope when I remember this: The faithful love of the LORD never ends!
LAMENTATIONS 3:1, 7–8, 21–22 NLT

But I tell you to love your enemies and pray for anyone who mistreats you.
MATTHEW 5:44 CEV

On days when life is difficult and I feel overwhelmed, as I do fairly often, it helps to remember in my prayers that all God requires of me is to trust Him and be His friend. I find I can do that.
BRUCE LARSON

Rejoice in hope, be patient in tribulation, be constant in prayer.
ROMANS 12:12 ESV

"But when you pray, go into your room, close the door and pray to your Father, who is unseen. Then your Father, who sees what is done in secret, will reward you. And when you pray, do not keep on babbling like pagans, for they think they will be heard because of their many words. Do not be like them, for your Father knows what you need before you ask him."
MATTHEW 6:6–8 NIV

"This, then, is how you should pray: 'Our Father in heaven, hallowed be your name, your kingdom come, your will be done, on earth as it is in heaven. Give us today our daily bread. And forgive us our debts, as we also have forgiven our debtors. And lead us not into temptation, but deliver us from the evil one.' "
MATTHEW 6:9–13 NIV

"And all things you ask in prayer, believing, you will receive."
MATTHEW 21:22 NASB

Invariable "success" in prayer would not prove the Christian doctrine at all. It would prove something more like magic—a power in certain human beings to control, or compel, the course of nature.

C. S. LEWIS

Is anyone among you in trouble? Let them pray. Is anyone happy? Let them sing songs of praise. Is anyone among you sick? Let them call the elders of the church to pray over them and anoint them with oil in the name of the Lord. And the prayer offered in faith will make the sick person well; the Lord will raise them up. If they have sinned, they will be forgiven. Therefore confess your sins to each other and pray for each other so that you may be healed. The prayer of a righteous person is powerful and effective.

JAMES 5:13–16 NIV

Husbands, likewise, dwell with them with understanding, giving honor to the wife, as to the weaker vessel, and as being heirs together of the grace of life, that your prayers may not be hindered.

1 PETER 3:7 NKJV

53

Pride

Want power and strength? Rid yourself of
pride. For only when we realize our own
weakness and come to Him humbly, does
God give us His might and muscle, ensuring
victory. Now that's a power surge!

"I, the LORD, will punish the world for its evil and the wicked for their sin. I will crush the arrogance of the proud and humble the pride of the mighty."
ISAIAH 13:11 NLT

The LORD will tear down the house of the proud, but He will establish the boundary of the widow.
PROVERBS 15:25 NASB

> *There is something within the human spirit that wants to resist the thought of weakness. Many times this is nothing more than our human pride at work. Just as weakness carries a great potential for strength, pride carries an equally great potential for defeat.*
> CHARLES STANLEY

The eyes of the arrogant will be humbled and human pride brought low; the LORD alone will be exalted in that day.
ISAIAH 2:11 NIV

"The fear of the LORD is to hate evil; pride and arrogance and the evil way and the perverse mouth I hate."
PROVERBS 8:13 NKJV

How blessed is the man who has made the LORD his trust, and has not turned to the proud, nor to those who lapse into falsehood.
PSALM 40:4 NASB

Believers in humble circumstances ought to take pride in their high position. But the rich should take pride in their humiliation— since they will pass away like a wild flower.
JAMES 1:9–10 NIV

Pride is to character, like the attic to the house—
the highest part, and generally the most empty.
SYDNEY HOWARD GAY

Too much pride can put you to shame. It's wiser to be humble.
PROVERBS 11:2 CEV

Finishing is better than starting. Patience is better than pride.
ECCLESIASTES 7:8 NLT

Where there is strife, there is pride, but wisdom is found in those
who take advice.
PROVERBS 13:10 NIV

If I had only one sermon to preach it would be a sermon against pride.
G. K. CHESTERTON

Pride goes before destruction, and haughtiness before a fall.
PROVERBS 16:18 NLT

In his pride the wicked man does not seek him;
in all his thoughts there is no room for God.
PSALM 10:4 NIV

Mockers are proud and haughty;
they act with boundless arrogance.
PROVERBS 21:24 NLT

God created the world out of nothing;
so as long as we are nothing, he can make something out of us.
MARTIN LUTHER

54

Salvation

Women are born multitaskers and capable of
astounding feats (like childbirth), but we're
powerless to save ourselves from our wrongdoing,
broken relationships, darkness, and judgment.
For that we need a Savior named Jesus. Only He
can rescue us from fire, flood, and storm, giving
us the peace, protection, and strength to love
and live the abundant life—now and forever!

" 'So I will save you, and you shall be a blessing. Do not fear, let your hands be strong.' "
ZECHARIAH 8:13 NKJV

Jesus is " 'the stone you builders rejected, which has become the cornerstone.' Salvation is found in no one else, for there is no other name under heaven given to mankind by which we must be saved."
ACTS 4:11–12 NIV

"The LORD is my strength and song, and He has become my salvation; He is my God, and I will praise Him; my father's God, and I will exalt Him."
EXODUS 15:2 NKJV

The LORD has made known His salvation; He has revealed His righteousness in the sight of the nations.
PSALM 98:2 NASB

For the LORD takes delight in his people;
he crowns the humble with victory.
PSALM 149:4 NIV

Safety does not depend on our conception of the absence of danger.
Safety is found in God's presence, in the center of His perfect will.
T. J. BACH

"My God is my rock, in whom I find protection. He is my shield, the power that saves me, and my place of safety. He is my refuge, my savior, the one who saves me from violence."
2 SAMUEL 22:3 NLT

I trust in your unfailing love; my heart rejoices in your salvation.
PSALM 13:5 NIV

The only thing of our very own which we contribute to our salvation is the sin which makes it necessary.
WILLIAM TEMPLE

Salvation is far from the wicked, for they do not seek Your statutes.
PSALM 119:155 NKJV

For I am not ashamed of the gospel, for it is the power of God for salvation to everyone who believes, to the Jew first and also to the Greek.
ROMANS 1:16 ESV

As God's partners, we beg you not to accept this marvelous gift of God's kindness and then ignore it. For God says, "At just the right time, I heard you. On the day of salvation, I helped you." Indeed, the "right time" is now. Today is the day of salvation.
2 CORINTHIANS 6:1–2 NLT

And you also were included in Christ when you heard the message of truth, the gospel of your salvation. When you believed, you were marked in him with a seal, the promised Holy Spirit, who is a deposit guaranteeing our inheritance until the redemption of those who are God's possession—to the praise of his glory.
EPHESIANS 1:13–14 NIV

Jesus didn't save you so you could cruise to heaven in a luxury liner. He wants you to be useful in His kingdom! The moment you got saved, He enrolled you in His school— the school of suffering and affliction.
DAVID WILKERSON

Therefore, my beloved, as you have always obeyed, not as in my presence only, but now much more in my absence, work out your own salvation with fear and trembling; for it is God who works in you both to will and to do for His good pleasure.

PHILIPPIANS 2:12–13 NKJV

Like newborn babies, crave pure spiritual milk, so that by it you may grow up in your salvation, now that you have tasted that the Lord is good.

1 PETER 2:2–3 NIV

"Lift up your eyes to the sky, then look to the earth beneath; for the sky will vanish like smoke, and the earth will wear out like a garment and its inhabitants will die in like manner; but My salvation will be forever, and My righteousness will not wane."

ISAIAH 51:6 NASB

> *God is none other than the Savior of our wretchedness.*
> *So we can only know God well by knowing our iniquities. . . .*
> *Those who have known God without knowing their wretchedness*
> *have not glorified Him, but have glorified themselves.*
> BLAISE PASCAL

And inasmuch as it is appointed for men to die once and after this comes judgment, so Christ also, having been offered once to bear the sins of many, will appear a second time for salvation without reference to sin, to those who eagerly await Him.

HEBREWS 9:27–28 NASB

55

Seeking God

Oftentimes we are so busy taking care of the
house and family, as well as working inside or
outside the home, that we neglect seeking God
and His will for our lives. Time to change up,
ladies! With faith in hand, seek Him today—
and every day. In doing so, your life will be
blessed, your heart full of praise. It's all good!

"But from there you will seek the LORD your God, and you will find Him if you seek Him with all your heart and with all your soul."
DEUTERONOMY 4:29 NKJV

Many have sought the Lord but not found Him because they failed to seek Him with their whole heart.
BILL GOTHARD

Glory in His holy name; let the heart of those who seek the LORD be glad. Seek the LORD and His strength; seek His face continually.
1 CHRONICLES 16:10–11 NASB

"Know the God of your father, and serve Him with a whole heart and a willing mind; for the LORD searches all hearts, and understands every intent of the thoughts. If you seek Him, He will let you find Him; but if you forsake Him, He will reject you forever."
1 CHRONICLES 28:9 NASB

Though God has no other desire than to impart Himself to the loving soul that seeks Him, yet He frequently conceals Himself from it, that it may be roused from sloth, and impelled to seek Him with fidelity and love.
MADAME JEANNE GUYON

"Then if my people who are called by my name will humble themselves and pray and seek my face and turn from their wicked ways, I will hear from heaven and will forgive their sins and restore their land."
2 CHRONICLES 7:14 NLT

Seek the Lord while he may be found; call on him while he is near.
ISAIAH 55:6 NIV

Hezekiah prayed for them, saying, "May the LORD, who is good, pardon everyone who sets their heart on seeking God—the LORD, the God of their ancestors—even if they are not clean according to the rules of the sanctuary." And the LORD heard Hezekiah and healed the people.
2 CHRONICLES 30:18–20 NIV

He who seeks God in tangible form misses the very thing he is seeking, for God is a Spirit.
HENRY DRUMMOND

From heaven the LORD looks down to see if anyone is wise enough to search for him.
PSALM 14:2 CEV

Those who know your name trust in you, for you, O LORD, do not abandon those who search for you.
PSALM 9:10 NLT

All over the world, people go to unimaginable lengths to find God— which is sad when you consider the unimaginable lengths God has already gone to find us.
JOANNA WEAVER

The one thing I ask of the LORD—the thing I seek most—is to live in the house of the LORD all the days of my life, delighting in the LORD's perfections and meditating in his Temple.
PSALM 27:4 NLT

My heart has heard you say, "Come and talk with me." And my heart responds, "LORD, I am coming."
PSALM 27:8 NLT

If you have an honest heart, an appetite for truth, and an openness to God's Spirit, you will be gratified by the results.
JOSH MCDOWELL AND DALE BELLIS

"I love those who love me, and those who seek me diligently will find me."
PROVERBS 8:17 NKJV

Every person, on coming to the knowledge of himself, is not only urged to seek God, but is also led as by the hand to find Him.
JOHN CALVIN

"But seek first the kingdom of God and His righteousness, and all these things shall be added to you."
MATTHEW 6:33 NKJV

"God did this so that they would seek him and perhaps reach out for him and find him, though he is not far from any one of us. 'For in him we live and move and have our being.' "
ACTS 17:27–28 NIV

Lord, I am a woman after Your heart. I seek Your face, guidance, love. Be with me now, Lord. I am ready, willing, and able to abide in Your presence.

And it is impossible to please God without faith. Anyone who wants to come to him must believe that God exists and that he rewards those who sincerely seek him.
HEBREWS 11:6 NLT

The process of seeking the Lord with our whole heart really begins with delighting in the Word of God.
BILL GOTHARD

56

Sexuality

God's plan was to join one man to one woman
and for them to desire and remain faithful to
each other. Stay true to your man. Make time
to just cuddle. Keep those home fires burning,
fulfilling your mutual desires. Allow him to
rejoice in your body. Remember, the love between
you and your spouse is as sacred as your love for
God. After all, it is called "holy matrimony."

And the LORD God said, "It is not good that man should be alone;
I will make him a helper comparable to him."
GENESIS 2:18 NKJV

There is not enough celebration of companionship.
Relationships aren't just about eroticism and sexuality.
FRANCESCA ANNIS

So God created mankind in his own image, in the image of God
he created them; male and female he created them. God blessed
them and said to them, "Be fruitful and increase in number;
fill the earth and subdue it."
GENESIS 1:27–28 NIV

Do not want anything that belongs to someone else.
Don't want anyone's house, wife or husband, slaves, oxen,
donkeys or anything else.
EXODUS 20:17 CEV

"If a man seduces a virgin who is not pledged to be married
and sleeps with her, he must pay the bride-price,
and she shall be his wife."
EXODUS 22:16 NIV

Nothing is more noble, nothing more venerable than fidelity.
Faithfulness and truth are the most sacred excellences and
endowments of the human mind.
MARCUS TULLIUS CICERO

Let your wife be a fountain of blessing for you. Rejoice in the wife
of your youth. She is a loving deer, a graceful doe. Let her breasts
satisfy you always. May you always be captivated by her love.
PROVERBS 5:18–19 NLT

My beloved spoke, and said to me:
"Rise up, my love, my fair one, and come away."
Song of Solomon 2:10 nkjv

'Tis easier to suppress the first desire, than to satisfy all that follow it.
Benjamin Franklin

Let us behave properly as in the day, not in carousing and
drunkenness, not in sexual promiscuity and sensuality,
not in strife and jealousy.
Romans 13:13 nasb

"I have the right to do anything," you say—but not everything
is beneficial. "I have the right to do anything"—but I will not be
mastered by anything. You say, "Food for the stomach and the
stomach for food, and God will destroy them both." The body,
however, is not meant for sexual immorality but for the Lord,
and the Lord for the body.
1 Corinthians 6:12–13 niv

For of this sort are those who creep into households and make
captives of gullible women loaded down with sins,
led away by various lusts.
2 Timothy 3:6 nkjv

*He who truly believes that which prompts him to an action has looked
upon the action to lust after it, he has committed it already in his heart.*
William Kingdon Clifford

I say then: Walk in the Spirit, and you shall not fulfill
the lust of the flesh.
Galatians 5:16 nkjv

Whoever sins sexually, sins against their own body. Do you not know that your bodies are temples of the Holy Spirit, who is in you, whom you have received from God? You are not your own; you were bought at a price. Therefore honor God with your bodies.

1 CORINTHIANS 6:18–20 NIV

Let the husband render to his wife the affection due her, and likewise also the wife to her husband. The wife does not have authority over her own body, but the husband does. And likewise the husband does not have authority over his own body, but the wife does. Do not deprive one another except with consent for a time, that you may give yourselves to fasting and prayer; and come together again so that Satan does not tempt you because of your lack of self-control.

1 CORINTHIANS 7:3–5 NKJV

It is love rather than sexual lust or unbridled sexuality if, in addition to the need or want involved, there is also some impulse to give pleasure to the persons thus loved and not merely to use them for our own selfish pleasure.

MORTIMER ADLER

God wants you to be holy and to stay away from sexual sins. He wants each of you to learn to control your own body in a way that is holy and honorable. Don't use your body for sexual sin like the people who do not know God.

1 THESSALONIANS 4:3–5 NCV

Sexuality is a private matter; some believe that broadcasting it destroys the very things that make it sacred.

LANCE LOUD

Each man must love his wife as he loves himself, and the wife must respect her husband.

EPHESIANS 5:33 NLT

Love grows. Lust wastes by enjoyment, and the reason is,
that one springs from a union of souls,
and the other from a union of sense.

WILLIAM PENN

So put all evil things out of your life: sexual sinning, doing evil, letting evil thoughts control you, wanting things that are evil, and greed. This is really serving a false god.

COLOSSIANS 3:5 NCV

No temptation has overtaken you but such as is common to man; and God is faithful, who will not allow you to be tempted beyond what you are able, but with the temptation will provide the way of escape also, so that you will be able to endure it.

1 CORINTHIANS 10:13 NASB

Give honor to marriage, and remain faithful to one another in marriage. God will surely judge people who are immoral and those who commit adultery.

HEBREWS 13:4 NLT

The more we are filled with thoughts of lust
the less we find true romantic love.

DOUGLAS HORTON

57

Sin

Sin entered the world when Eve bit into the
serpent's cunning, his master lie being "You will
be like God." Ever since then, our wrongdoings
or sins have separated us from the Lord. But
we can rejoice in the fact that Jesus' death
reconciles us to God. Oh, what a Savior! So,
instead of hiding your sins from God, confess
them. God's ready, willing, and able to forgive.

The Lord passed in front of Moses, calling out, "Yahweh! The Lord! The God of compassion and mercy! I am slow to anger and filled with unfailing love and faithfulness. I lavish unfailing love to a thousand generations. I forgive iniquity, rebellion, and sin. But I do not excuse the guilty. I lay the sins of the parents upon their children and grandchildren; the entire family is affected—even children in the third and fourth generations."
Exodus 34:6–7 NLT

Sin is wrong, not because of what it does to me, or my spouse, or child, or neighbor, but because it is an act of rebellion against the infinitely holy and majestic God.
Jerry Bridges

Be gracious to me, O God, according to Your lovingkindness; according to the greatness of Your compassion blot out my transgressions. Wash me thoroughly from my iniquity and cleanse me from my sin. For I know my transgressions, and my sin is ever before me. Against You, You only, I have sinned and done what is evil in Your sight, so that You are justified when You speak and blameless when You judge.
Psalm 51:1–4 NASB

[Jesus] himself bore our sins in his body on the tree, that we might die to sin and live to righteousness. By his wounds you have been healed.
1 Peter 2:24 ESV

The next day [John the Baptist] saw Jesus coming toward him, and said, "Behold, the Lamb of God, who takes away the sin of the world!"
John 1:29 ESV

Behold, I was brought forth in iniquity, and in sin my mother conceived me.
PSALM 51:5 NKJV

The wages of the righteous is life, the income of the wicked, punishment.
PROVERBS 10:16 NASB

Therefore, just as sin came into the world through one man, and death through sin, and so death spread to all men because all sinned—for sin indeed was in the world before the law was given, but sin is not counted where there is no law.
ROMANS 5:12–13 ESV

> *Jesus was God and man in one person,*
> *that God and man might be happy together again.*
> GEORGE WHITEFIELD

For He made Him who knew no sin to be sin for us, that we might become the righteousness of God in Him.
2 CORINTHIANS 5:21 NKJV

Jesus replied, "I tell you the truth, everyone who sins is a slave of sin."
JOHN 8:34 NLT

For a man's ways are before the eyes of the LORD, and he ponders all his paths. The iniquities of the wicked ensnare him, and he is held fast in the cords of his sin.
PROVERBS 5:21–23 ESV

We know that the Law is spiritual. But I am merely a human, and I have been sold as a slave to sin. In fact, I don't understand why I act the way I do. I don't do what I know is right. I do the things I hate. Although I don't do what I know is right, I agree that the Law is good. So I am not the one doing these evil things. The sin that lives in me is what does them. I know that my selfish desires won't let me do anything that is good. Even when I want to do right, I cannot. Instead of doing what I know is right, I do wrong.

ROMANS 7:14–19 CEV

No one who abides in him keeps on sinning; no one who keeps on sinning has either seen him or known him.

1 JOHN 3:6 ESV

When [Jesus] died, he died once to break the power of sin. But now that he lives, he lives for the glory of God. So you also should consider yourselves to be dead to the power of sin and alive to God through Christ Jesus. Do not let sin control the way you live; do not give in to sinful desires. Do not let any part of your body become an instrument of evil to serve sin. Instead, give yourselves completely to God, for you were dead, but now you have new life. So use your whole body as an instrument to do what is right for the glory of God. Sin is no longer your master, for you no longer live under the requirements of the law. Instead, you live under the freedom of God's grace.

ROMANS 6:10–14 NLT

We must learn where our personal weaknesses lie. Once they are identified, we must be ruthless in dealing with them.

ALISTAIR BEGG

What then? Shall we sin because we are not under law but under grace? May it never be! Do you not know that when you present yourselves to someone as slaves for obedience, you are slaves of the one whom you obey, either of sin resulting in death, or of obedience resulting in righteousness? But thanks be to God that though you were slaves of sin, you became obedient from the heart to that form of teaching to which you were committed, and having been freed from sin, you became slaves of righteousness.
ROMANS 6:15–18 NASB

But now that you have been set free from sin and have become slaves of God, the fruit you get leads to sanctification and its end, eternal life. For the wages of sin is death, but the free gift of God is eternal life in Christ Jesus our Lord.
ROMANS 6:22–24 ESV

After grief for sin, there should be joy for forgiveness.
A. W. PINK

For while we were living in the flesh, our sinful passions, aroused by the law, were at work in our members to bear fruit for death. But now we are released from the law, having died to that which held us captive, so that we serve in the new way of the Spirit and not in the old way of the written code.
ROMANS 7:5–6 ESV

But each of you had better tremble and turn from your sins. Silently search your heart as you lie in bed.
PSALM 4:4 CEV

And if Christ is in you, the body is dead because of sin, but the Spirit is life because of righteousness.
ROMANS 8:10 NKJV

Flee from sexual immorality. All other sins a person commits are outside the body, but whoever sins sexually, sins against their own body.
1 Corinthians 6:18 niv

It does not spoil your happiness to confess your sin.
The unhappiness is in not making the confession.
C. H. Spurgeon

If we confess our sins, he is faithful and just to forgive us our sins, and to cleanse us from all unrighteousness.
1 John 1:9 kjv

I have hidden your word in my heart that I might not sin against you.
Psalm 119:11 niv

Therefore, dear brothers and sisters, you have no obligation to do what your sinful nature urges you to do. For if you live by its dictates, you will die. But if through the power of the Spirit you put to death the deeds of your sinful nature, you will live. For all who are led by the Spirit of God are children of God.
Romans 8:12–14 nlt

Then Peter came to Jesus and asked, "Lord, how many times shall I forgive my brother or sister who sins against me? Up to seven times?" Jesus answered, "I tell you, not seven times, but seventy-seven times."
Matthew 18:21–22 niv

Righteousness exalts a nation, but sin is a reproach to any people.
Proverbs 14:34 nkjv

58

Spiritual Fruit

Unless we are abiding in Christ, we can do
nothing. But when we live in Him, we are
complete and able to bear all kinds of good
spiritual fruit. So live by the Spirit, girl!
You'll be amazed at the harvest! Peachy!

But the fruit of the Spirit is love, joy, peace, longsuffering, kindness, goodness, faithfulness, gentleness, self-control. Against such there is no law.
GALATIANS 5:22–23 NKJV

Blessed is the one who does not walk in step with the wicked or stand in the way that sinners take or sit in the company of mockers, but whose delight is in the law of the LORD, and who meditates on his law day and night. That person is like a tree planted by streams of water, which yields its fruit in season and whose leaf does not wither—whatever they do prospers.
PSALM 1:1–3 NIV

"Beware of false prophets who come disguised as harmless sheep but are really vicious wolves. You can identify them by their fruit, that is, by the way they act. Can you pick grapes from thornbushes, or figs from thistles? A good tree produces good fruit, and a bad tree produces bad fruit."
MATTHEW 7:15–17 NLT

God develops the fruit of the Spirit in your life by allowing you to experience circumstances in which you're tempted to express the exact opposite quality. Character development always involves a choice, and temptation provides that opportunity.
RICK WARREN

You did not choose me. I chose you and sent you out to produce fruit, the kind of fruit that will last. Then my Father will give you whatever you ask for in my name.
JOHN 15:16 CEV

"Remain in me, as I also remain in you. No branch can bear fruit by itself; it must remain in the vine. Neither can you bear fruit unless you remain in me. I am the vine; you are the branches. If you remain in me and I in you, you will bear much fruit; apart from me you can do nothing. If you do not remain in me, you are like a branch that is thrown away and withers; such branches are picked up, thrown into the fire and burned."
JOHN 15:4–6 NIV

Likewise, my brothers, you also have died to the law through the body of Christ, so that you may belong to another, to him who has been raised from the dead, in order that we may bear fruit for God.
ROMANS 7:4 ESV

The fruit of the Spirit is not push, drive, climb, grasp and trample. . . .
Life is more than a climb to the top of the heap.
RICHARD J. FOSTER

For you were once darkness, but now you are light in the Lord. Live as children of light (for the fruit of the light consists in all goodness, righteousness and truth) and find out what pleases the Lord.
EPHESIANS 5:8–10 NIV

The Christian personality is hidden deep inside us. It is unseen, like the soup carried in a tureen high over a waiter's head. No one knows what's inside—unless the waiter is bumped and he trips! Just so, people don't know what's inside us until we've been bumped. But if Christ is living inside, what spills out is the fruit of the Spirit.
HENRY WINGBLADE

59

Spiritual Gifts

God has equipped each and every one of us with spiritual gifts we are to use in service to others. So don't be a pew potato. Find out what talent God has in mind for you, then use it to enhance the body of Christ. It does a body good!

But the manifestation of the Spirit is given to each one for the profit of all: for to one is given the word of wisdom through the Spirit, to another the word of knowledge through the same Spirit, to another faith by the same Spirit, to another gifts of healings by the same Spirit, to another the working of miracles, to another prophecy, to another discerning of spirits, to another different kinds of tongues, to another the interpretation of tongues. But one and the same Spirit works all these things, distributing to each one individually as He wills.
1 Corinthians 12:7–11 nkjv

Now there are varieties of gifts, but the same Spirit.
1 Corinthians 12:4–5 esv

For I say, through the grace given to me, to everyone who is among you, not to think of himself more highly than he ought to think, but to think soberly, as God has dealt to each one a measure of faith. For as we have many members in one body, but all the members do not have the same function, so we, being many, are one body in Christ, and individually members of one another. Having then gifts differing according to the grace that is given to us, let us use them: if prophecy, let us prophesy in proportion to our faith; or ministry, let us use it in our ministering; he who teaches, in teaching; he who exhorts, in exhortation; he who gives, with liberality; he who leads, with diligence; he who shows mercy, with cheerfulness.
Romans 12:3–8 nkjv

And God has placed in the church first of all apostles, second prophets, third teachers, then miracles, then gifts of healing, of helping, of guidance, and of different kinds of tongues.
1 Corinthians 12:28 niv

60

Spiritual Refreshment

The hectic pace of society, the seemingly never-ending needs of friends and family, and the woes of this world are enough to make any woman weary. Thank God He's given us the Word with which we can find rest and refreshment. Take time each day to be still in God's presence, allowing Him to give you an extreme makeover—body, mind, and soul.

For this is what the high and exalted One says—he who lives forever, whose name is holy: "I live in a high and holy place, but also with the one who is contrite and lowly in spirit, to revive the spirit of the lowly and to revive the heart of the contrite."
Isaiah 57:15 NIV

I drove away from my mind everything capable of spoiling the sense of the presence of God. . . . I just make it my business to persevere in His holy presence. . . . My soul has had a habitual, silent, secret conversation with God.
BROTHER LAWRENCE

" 'Therefore the people of Israel shall keep the Sabbath, observing the Sabbath throughout their generations, as a covenant forever. It is a sign forever between me and the people of Israel that in six days the LORD made heaven and earth, and on the seventh day he rested and was refreshed.' "
Exodus 31:16–17 ESV

Trust in the LORD with all your heart, and lean not on your own understanding; in all your ways acknowledge Him, and He shall direct your paths. Do not be wise in your own eyes; fear the LORD and depart from evil. It will be health to your flesh, and strength to your bones.
Proverbs 3:5–8 NKJV

Revival is not just an emotional touch; it's a complete takeover!
NANCY LEIGH DeMOSS

"Repent, then, and turn to God, so that your sins may be wiped out, that times of refreshing may come from the Lord, and that he may send the Messiah, who has been appointed for you—even Jesus."
Acts 3:19–20 NIV

In the silences I make in the midst of the turmoil of life, I have appointments with God. From these silences, I come forth with spirit refreshed, and with a renewed sense of power. I hear a voice in the silences, and become increasingly aware that it is the voice of God.
DAVID BRAINERD

I will praise the name of God with a song; I will magnify him with thanksgiving. . . . When the humble see it they will be glad; you who seek God, let your hearts revive. For the LORD hears the needy and does not despise his own people who are prisoners.
PSALM 69:30, 32–33 ESV

I rejoice over the coming of Stephanas and Fortunatus and Achaicus, because they have supplied what was lacking on your part. For they have refreshed my spirit and yours. Therefore acknowledge such men.
1 CORINTHIANS 16:17–18 NASB

Therefore we have been comforted in your comfort. And we rejoiced exceedingly more for the joy of Titus, because his spirit has been refreshed by you all.
2 CORINTHIANS 7:13 NKJV

[Lord,] will You not revive us again, that Your people may rejoice in You?
PSALM 85:6 NKJV

61

stress

Women are more susceptible to stress than men because many of us are trying to juggle various roles as we strive to be perfect employees, mothers, daughters, and wives. Not to mention getting periodically zapped by hormonal changes due to childbirth, menstruation, and menopause. But take heart! Drinking in God's presence, feeding on His Word, and taking a nice hot bath are perfect stress reducers. Learning to say "no" wouldn't hurt either!

Without the help of the LORD it is useless to build a home or to guard a city. It is useless to get up early and stay up late in order to earn a living. God takes care of his own, even while they sleep.
PSALM 127:1–2 CEV

And the angel of the LORD came back the second time, and touched him, and said, "Arise and eat, because the journey is too great for you." So he arose, and ate and drank; and he went in the strength of that food forty days and forty nights as far as Horeb, the mountain of God.
1 KINGS 19:7–8 NKJV

"The seed cast in the weeds represents the ones who hear the kingdom news but are overwhelmed with worries about all the things they have to do and all the things they want to get. The stress strangles what they heard, and nothing comes of it."
MARK 4:18–19 MSG

Lord, the stress in life is choking out my joy. Show me what You would have me do this day and help me to say "no" when I need to.

Give your burdens to the LORD, and he will take care of you.
He will not permit the godly to slip and fall.
PSALM 55:22 NLT

My heart is troubled and does not rest;
days of affliction come to meet me.
JOB 30:27 AMP

A women under stress is not immediately concerned with finding solutions to her problems but rather seeks relief by expressing herself and being understood.
JOHN GRAY

"Martha, Martha," the Lord answered, "you are worried and upset about many things, but few things are needed—or indeed only one. Mary has chosen what is better, and it will not be taken away from her."
Luke 10:41–42 niv

But more than anything else, put God's work first and do what he wants. Then the other things will be yours as well.
Matthew 6:33 cev

Many of those who once were so passionately in love with Christ now run about pursuing their own interests. They're burdened down with stress and problems, chasing after riches and the things of this world.
David Wilkerson

"Get away with me and you'll recover your life. I'll show you how to take a real rest. Walk with me and work with me—watch how I do it. Learn the unforced rhythms of grace. I won't lay anything heavy or ill-fitting on you. Keep company with me and you'll learn to live freely and lightly."
Matthew 11:28–30 msg

Stress is an ignorant state. It believes that everything is an emergency. Nothing is that important. Just lie down.
Natalie Goldberg

"A bruised reed he will not break, and a smoldering wick he will not snuff out, till he has brought justice through to victory."
Matthew 12:20 niv

"Don't let your hearts be troubled. Trust in God, and trust also in me."
John 14:1 nlt

Each day that we live, he provides for our needs and gives us the strength of a young eagle.

Psalm 103:5 CEV

Adopting the right attitude can convert
a negative stress into a positive one.

Hans Selye

"Why work for something that doesn't really satisfy you? Listen closely to me, and you will eat what is good; your soul will enjoy the rich food that satisfies. Come to me and listen; listen to me so you may live."

Isaiah 55:2–3 NCV

"Don't be afraid, for I am with you. Don't be discouraged, for I am your God. I will strengthen you and help you. I will hold you up with my victorious right hand."

Isaiah 41:10 NLT

I will boast all the more gladly about my weaknesses, so that Christ's power may rest on me. That is why, for Christ's sake, I delight in weaknesses, in insults, in hardships, in persecutions, in difficulties. For when I am weak, then I am strong.

2 Corinthians 12:9–10 NIV

There may be no olives growing and no food growing in the fields. There may be no sheep in the pens and no cattle in the barns. But I will still be glad in the Lord; I will rejoice in God my Savior. The Lord God is my strength. He makes me like a deer that does not stumble so I can walk on the steep mountains.

Habakkuk 3:17–19 NCV

62

Success

Worldly success is measured in terms of
money and material possessions. But God
bases success on the intangibles—serving and
loving others, loving, seeking, and obeying
God, and delighting in His presence. Strive
for success with God alone, and you'll
prosper in every other area of your life.

"Only be strong and very courageous; be careful to do according to all the law which Moses My servant commanded you; do not turn from it to the right or to the left, so that you may have success wherever you go. This book of the law shall not depart from your mouth, but you shall meditate on it day and night, so that you may be careful to do according to all that is written in it; for then you will make your way prosperous, and then you will have success."

JOSHUA 1:7–8 NASB

"Therefore keep the words of this covenant and do them, that you may prosper in all that you do."

DEUTERONOMY 29:9 ESV

Blessed is the one who does not walk in step with the wicked or stand in the way that sinners take or sit in the company of mockers, but whose delight is in the law of the LORD, and who meditates on his law day and night. That person is like a tree planted by streams of water, which yields its fruit in season and whose leaf does not wither—whatever they do prospers.

PSALM 1:1–3 NIV

There are great positives as well as refusals necessary for him who would find real prosperity. He must not only say no to the wrong, he must say yes to the right. He must not only avoid the seat of the scornful, but his delight must be in the law of the Lord.

CLOVIS G. CHAPPELL

Who is the man who fears the LORD? He will instruct him in the way he should choose. His soul will abide in prosperity, and his descendants will inherit the land. The secret of the LORD is for those who fear Him, and He will make them know His covenant.

PSALM 25:12–14 NASB

The LORD was with Joseph so that he prospered, and he lived
in the house of his Egyptian master. When his master saw that
the LORD was with him and that the LORD gave him success in
everything he did, Joseph found favor in his eyes and became his
attendant. Potiphar put him in charge of his household, and he
entrusted to his care everything he owned.
GENESIS 39:2–4 NIV

David continued to succeed in everything he did, for the LORD
was with him.
1 SAMUEL 18:14 NLT

[King Hezekiah] trusted in the LORD, the God of Israel, so that
there was none like him among all the kings of Judah after
him, nor among those who were before him. For he held fast
to the LORD. He did not depart from following him, but kept the
commandments that the LORD commanded Moses. And the LORD
was with him; wherever he went out, he prospered. He rebelled
against the king of Assyria and would not serve him.
2 KINGS 18:5–7 ESV

*Before Nehemiah spoke to King Artaxerxes about rebuilding Jerusalem,
he prayed for success in bringing his case before the king. There is
nothing we cannot ask God for, as long as we are seeking His will.*

"Lord, let your ear be attentive to the prayer of this your servant
and to the prayer of your servants who delight in revering your
name. Give your servant success today by granting him favor in
the presence of this man." I was cupbearer to the king.
NEHEMIAH 1:11 NIV

Save now, I pray, O LORD; O LORD, I pray, send now prosperity.
PSALM 118:25 NKJV

Being humble involves the willingness to be reckoned a failure
in everyone's sight but God's.
ROY M. PEARSON

Now in my prosperity I said, "I shall never be moved."
LORD, by Your favor You have made my mountain stand strong;
You hid Your face, and I was troubled.
PSALM 30:6–7 NKJV

Faith is often strengthened right at the place of disappointment.
RODNEY MCBRIDE

Enjoy prosperity while you can, but when hard times strike,
realize that both come from God. Remember that nothing is
certain in this life.
ECCLESIASTES 7:14 NLT

"Terrors are turned against me; they pursue my honor as the
wind, and my prosperity has passed away like a cloud."
JOB 30:15 NASB

Rest in the LORD, and wait patiently for Him; do not fret because
of him who prospers in his way, because of the man who brings
wicked schemes to pass.
PSALM 37:7 NKJV

He who conceals his transgressions will not prosper, but he who
confesses and forsakes them will find compassion.
PROVERBS 28:13 NASB

But the soul renounced shall abide in the boundlessness of God's life.
This is liberty, this is prosperity. The more we lose, the more we gain.
WATCHMAN NEE

63

Temptation

Mmm. Chocolate. A mighty temptress. As is a new pair of shoes or purse. It's hard to resist satiating our appetite for things that make us feel good in the moment but guilty in the long run. These selfish desires make us easy prey for the ultimate tempter, Satan. But God would have us resist the father of lies. Ask Jesus for help. He'll lead you away from the evil one.

Don't blame God when you are tempted! God cannot be tempted
by evil, and he doesn't use evil to tempt others. We are tempted
by our own desires that drag us off and trap us. Our desires
make us sin, and when sin is finished with us, it leaves us dead.
JAMES 1:13–15 CEV

Because [Jesus] himself suffered when he was tempted,
he is able to help those who are being tempted.
HEBREWS 2:18 NIV

This High Priest of ours understands our weaknesses,
for he faced all of the same testings we do, yet he did not sin.
HEBREWS 4:15 NLT

If we do not abide in prayer, we will abide in temptation.
JOHN OWEN

"Watch and pray, lest you enter into temptation.
The spirit indeed is willing, but the flesh is weak."
MATTHEW 26:41 NKJV

*I cannot tell how I am buffeted sometimes by temptation. I never knew
how bad a heart I have. Yet I do know that I love God and love His
work, and desire to serve Him only and in all things. And I value
above all else that precious Saviour in whom alone I can be accepted.*
JAMES HUDSON TAYLOR

No temptation has overtaken you except what is common to
mankind. And God is faithful; he will not let you be tempted
beyond what you can bear. But when you are tempted,
he will also provide a way out so that you can endure it.
1 CORINTHIANS 10:13 NIV

Brethren, even if anyone is caught in any trespass, you who are spiritual, restore such a one in a spirit of gentleness; each one looking to yourself, so that you too will not be tempted.

GALATIANS 6:1 NASB

But those who desire to be rich fall into temptation, into a snare, into many senseless and harmful desires that plunge people into ruin and destruction.

1 TIMOTHY 6:9 ESV

Temptations, when we meet them at first, are as the lion that reared upon Samson; but if we overcome them, the next time we see them we shall find a nest of honey within them.

JOHN BUNYAN

Consider it a sheer gift, friends, when tests and challenges come at you from all sides. You know that under pressure, your faith-life is forced into the open and shows its true colors. So don't try to get out of anything prematurely. Let it do its work so you become mature and well-developed, not deficient in any way.

JAMES 1:2 MSG

Blessed is the one who perseveres under trial because, having stood the test, that person will receive the crown of life that the Lord has promised to those who love him. When tempted, no one should say, "God is tempting me." For God cannot be tempted by evil, nor does he tempt anyone; but each person is tempted when they are dragged away by their own evil desire and enticed.

JAMES 1:12–14 NIV

" 'Lead us not into temptation, but deliver us from the evil one.' "

MATTHEW 6:13 NIV

The Bible teaches us in times of temptation. . .there is one command:
Flee! Get away from it. . .for every struggle against lust in one's own
strength is doomed to failure.
DIETRICH BONHOEFFER

Run from temptations that capture young people. Always do the
right thing. Be faithful, loving, and easy to get along with.
Worship with people whose hearts are pure.
2 TIMOTHY 2:22 CEV

Flee from sexual immorality. All other sins a person commits are
outside the body, but whoever sins sexually, sins against
their own body.
1 CORINTHIANS 6:18 NIV

Do not deprive each other of sexual relations, unless you both
agree to refrain from sexual intimacy for a limited time so you can
give yourselves more completely to prayer. Afterward, you should
come together again so that Satan won't be able to tempt you
because of your lack of self-control.
1 CORINTHIANS 7:5 NLT

Submit therefore to God. Resist the devil
and he will flee from you.
JAMES 4:7 NASB

64

Thoughts

What we think influences what we do. That's why God is so interested in our mind-set. He wants our thoughts focused on Him. When they are, our actions will be right. So pay attention to your thoughts. Take them captive and yield them to Christ. He'll give us the proper mind-set. It's life transforming!

In his pride the wicked man does not seek him; in all his thoughts there is no room for God.
PSALM 10:4 NIV

Listen to my prayer, O God, do not ignore my plea; hear me and answer me. My thoughts trouble me and I am distraught.
PSALM 55:1–2 NIV

You don't have to control your thoughts;
you just have to stop letting them control you.
DAN MILLMAN

"For the thing I greatly feared has come upon me, and what I dreaded has happened to me."
JOB 3:25 NKJV

For as he thinketh in his heart, so is he.
PROVERBS 23:7 KJV

I've learned from experience that the greater part of our happiness or
misery depends on our dispositions and not on our circumstances.
MARTHA WASHINGTON

You have looked deep into my heart, LORD, and you know all about me. You know when I am resting or when I am working, and from heaven you discover my thoughts. You notice everything I do and everywhere I go.
PSALM 139:1–3 CEV

Search me, God, and know my heart;
test me and know my anxious thoughts.
PSALM 139:23 NIV

She does not ponder the path of life;
her ways are unstable, she does not know it.
PROVERBS 5:6 NASB

Give careful thought to the paths for your feet and be steadfast in
all your ways.
PROVERBS 4:26 NIV

Don't copy the behavior and customs of this world, but let God
transform you into a new person by changing the way you think.
Then you will learn to know God's will for you, which is good and
pleasing and perfect.
ROMANS 12:2 NLT

> *The greatest weapon against stress is our ability*
> *to choose one thought over another.*
> WILLIAM JAMES

And set your minds and keep them set on what is above
(the higher things), not on the things that are on the earth.
COLOSSIANS 3:2 AMP

"For My thoughts are not your thoughts, nor are your ways My
ways," says the LORD. "For as the heavens are higher than the
earth, so are My ways higher than your ways, and My thoughts
than your thoughts."
ISAIAH 55:8–9 NKJV

He who forms the mountains, who creates the wind, and who
reveals his thoughts to mankind, who turns dawn to darkness,
and treads on the heights of the earth—the LORD God Almighty
is his name.
AMOS 4:13 NIV

"For from within, out of a person's heart, come evil thoughts, sexual immorality, theft, murder, adultery, greed, wickedness, deceit, lustful desires, envy, slander, pride, and foolishness."
MARK 7:21–22 NLT

First comes thought; then organization of that thought, into ideas and plans; then transformation of those plans into reality. The beginning, as you will observe, is in your imagination.
NAPOLEON HILL

When she heard about Jesus, she came up behind him in the crowd and touched his cloak, because she thought, "If I just touch his clothes, I will be healed." Immediately her bleeding stopped and she felt in her body that she was freed from her suffering.
MARK 5:27–29 NIV

Change your thoughts and you change your world.
NORMAN VINCENT PEALE

So all of you holy brothers and sisters, who were called by God, think about Jesus, who was sent to us and is the high priest of our faith.
HEBREWS 3:1 NCV

For the word of God is alive and active. Sharper than any double-edged sword, it penetrates even to dividing soul and spirit, joints and marrow; it judges the thoughts and attitudes of the heart.
HEBREWS 4:12 NIV

65

Time Management

We sit down to eat a hot meal but before the fork enters our mouth the baby cries. Or we take out our Bible for devotions and our cell phone rings. Managing our time is all about priorities. As a general rule, a Christian woman's top six priorities are first God, then husband, children, work, prayer, and ministry. Try writing up your to-do lists with those guidelines in mind.

Good things happen when you get your priorities straight.
SCOTT CAAN

Follow God's example, therefore, as dearly loved children and walk in the way of love, just as Christ loved us and gave himself up for us as a fragrant offering and sacrifice to God.
EPHESIANS 5:1–2 NIV

And further, submit to one another out of reverence for Christ. For wives, this means submit to your husbands as to the Lord.
EPHESIANS 5:21–22 NLT

Parents, don't be hard on your children. Raise them properly. Teach them and instruct them about the Lord.
EPHESIANS 6:4 CEV

I did not like leaving them when they were little or big. You have to have priorities regarding what you will allow to take you away from your kid.
KATE HUDSON

As slaves of Christ, do the will of God with all your heart. Work with enthusiasm, as though you were working for the Lord rather than for people. Remember that the Lord will reward each one of us for the good we do, whether we are slaves or free.
EPHESIANS 6:6–8 NLT

We do not have a money problem in America. We have a values and priorities problem.
MARIAN WRIGHT EDELMAN

"She did what she could when she could."
MARK 14:8 MSG

Pray also for me, that whenever I speak, words may be given me so that I will fearlessly make known the mystery of the gospel, for which I am an ambassador in chains. Pray that I may declare it fearlessly, as I should.
EPHESIANS 6:19–20 NIV

Lord, give me wisdom as I review my to-dos today. Show me what You would have me do first. And help me carve out some downtime for myself.

The key is not to prioritize what's on your schedule, but to schedule your priorities.
STEPHEN COVEY

Don't be like the people of this world, but let God change the way you think. Then you will know how to do everything that is good and pleasing to him.
ROMANS 12:2 CEV

In a way, I have simplified my life by setting priorities.
KAREN DUFFY

They even did more than we had hoped, for their first action was to give themselves to the Lord and to us, just as God wanted them to do.
2 CORINTHIANS 8:5 NLT

But if a widow has children or grandchildren, these should learn first of all to put their religion into practice by caring for their own family and so repaying their parents and grandparents, for this is pleasing to God.
1 TIMOTHY 5:4 NIV

*I'm starting to judge success by the time I have for myself,
the time I spend with family and friends.
My priorities aren't amending; they're shifting.*
BRENDAN FRASER

Then Saul said, "Let's chase the Philistines all night and plunder
them until sunrise. Let's destroy every last one of them." His men
replied, "We'll do whatever you think is best." But the priest said,
"Let's ask God first."
1 SAMUEL 14:36 NLT

But more than anything else, put God's work first and do what he
wants. Then the other things will be yours as well.
MATTHEW 6:33 CEV

We also have to ask if we are focusing on the most important priorities.
FRED THOMPSON

It is good to praise the LORD and make music to your name,
O Most High, proclaiming your love in the morning and your
faithfulness at night.
PSALM 92:1–2 NIV

Trust the LORD with all your heart, and don't depend on your own
understanding. Remember the LORD in all you do, and he will
give you success.
PROVERBS 3:5–6 NCV

As soon as you enter a home, say, "God bless this home with
peace." If the people living there are peace-loving, your prayer
for peace will bless them. But if they are not peace-loving,
your prayer will return to you.
LUKE 10:5–6 CEV

66

Tongue

Women like to express themselves through words. But what words are we using? Are they encouraging or critical, truths or tales, gossip or good news? Remember, once our words are out there, there's no taking them back. What's on your tongue?

"The Spirit of the LORD spoke through me;
his word was on my tongue."
2 SAMUEL 23:2 NIV

"As long as I have life within me, the breath of God in my nostrils,
my lips will not say anything wicked, and my tongue
will not utter lies."
JOB 27:3–4 NIV

My heart overflows with a good theme; I address my verses to
the King; my tongue is the pen of a ready writer.
PSALM 45:1 NASB

*We have a natural right to make use of our pens as of our tongue,
at our peril, risk, and hazard.*
VOLTAIRE

LORD, who may enter your Holy Tent? Who may live on your holy
mountain? Only those who are innocent and who do what is
right. Such people speak the truth from their hearts and do not
tell lies about others. They do no wrong to their neighbors and
do not gossip.
PSALM 15:1–3 NCV

I said, "I will watch my ways and keep my tongue from sin; I will
put a muzzle on my mouth while in the presence of the wicked."
PSALM 39:1 NIV

*Lord, I know You hear every word that comes out of my mouth.
Please help me to always think before I speak.*

Kind words heal and help; cutting words wound and maim.
PROVERBS 15:4 MSG

The words of the reckless pierce like swords, but the tongue of the wise brings healing.
PROVERBS 12:18 NIV

Fighting is essentially a masculine idea;
a woman's weapon is her tongue.
HERMIONE GINGOLD

Before the tongue can speak, it must have lost the power to wound.
PEACE PILGRIM

Death and life are in the power of the tongue: and they that love it shall eat the fruit thereof.
PROVERBS 18:21 KJV

He who guards his mouth and his tongue,
guards his soul from troubles.
PROVERBS 21:23 NASB

A wife of noble character who can find? . . . She speaks with wisdom, and faithful instruction is on her tongue.
PROVERBS 31:10, 26 NIV

The Lord GOD has given me the tongue of those who are taught, that I may know how to sustain with a word him who is weary.
ISAIAH 50:4 ESV

Put a bridle on thy tongue; set a guard before thy lips, lest the words
of thine own mouth destroy thy peace. . .on much speaking cometh
repentance, but in silence is safety.
WILLIAM DRUMMOND

If you claim to be religious but don't control your tongue, you are fooling yourself, and your religion is worthless.
JAMES 1:26 NLT

And a small rudder makes a huge ship turn wherever the pilot chooses to go, even though the winds are strong. In the same way, the tongue is a small thing that makes grand speeches. But a tiny spark can set a great forest on fire.
JAMES 3:4–5 NLT

Fire and swords are slow engines of destruction, compared to the tongue of a gossip.
RICHARD STEELE

The tongue also is a fire, a world of evil among the parts of the body. It corrupts the whole body, sets the whole course of one's life on fire, and is itself set on fire by hell.
JAMES 3:6 NIV

No one can tame the tongue. It is restless and evil, full of deadly poison. Sometimes it praises our Lord and Father, and sometimes it curses those who have been made in the image of God. And so blessing and cursing come pouring out of the same mouth. Surely, my brothers and sisters, this is not right!
JAMES 3:8–10 NLT

All parts of the body get tired eventually—except the tongue.
KONRAD ADENAUER

67

Trust

People often let us down. After all, they're only human. But there is One you can always rely on— no matter what: God. You can trust Him to love, protect, and guide you. Need a rock and refuge? Look up to God. He'll never let you down.

"Do not put your trust in idols or make metal images of gods for yourselves. I am the LORD your God."
LEVITICUS 19:4 NLT

The LORD is a shelter for the oppressed, a refuge in times of trouble. Those who know your name trust in you, for you, O LORD, do not abandon those who search for you.
PSALM 9:9–10 NLT

The instructions of the LORD are perfect, reviving the soul. The decrees of the LORD are trustworthy, making wise the simple.
PSALM 19:7 NLT

Even strong young lions sometimes go hungry, but those who trust in the LORD will lack no good thing.
PSALM 34:10 NLT

Christ will make his home in your hearts as you trust in him. Your roots will grow down into God's love and keep you strong.
EPHESIANS 3:17 NLT

Faith, which is trust, and fear are opposite poles. If a man has the one, he can scarcely have the other in vigorous operation.
ALEXANDER MACLAREN

The LORD is my strength and my shield; in him my heart trusts, and I am helped; my heart exults, and with my song I give thanks to him.
PSALM 28:7 ESV

Many are the woes of the wicked, but the LORD's unfailing love surrounds the one who trusts in him.
PSALM 32:10 NIV

Commit your way to the LORD, trust also in Him,
and He shall bring it to pass.
PSALM 37:5 NKJV

Talk what we will of faith, if we do not trust and rely upon Him,
we do not believe in Him.
ANTONY FARINDON

I will not trust in my bow, nor will my sword save me. But You
have saved us from our adversaries, and You have put to shame
those who hate us.
PSALM 44:6–7 NASB

Whenever I am afraid, I will trust in You.
PSALM 56:3 NKJV

The creeping wilderness will soon take over that church that trusts in
its own strength and forgets to watch and pray.
A. W. TOZER

I will say of the LORD, "He is my refuge and my fortress,
my God, in whom I trust."
PSALM 91:2 NIV

Bad news won't bother [those who fear the Lord];
they have decided to trust the LORD.
PSALM 112:7 CEV

There are always uncertainties ahead, but there is always one
certainty—God's will is good.
VERNON PATERSON

68

Wisdom

Wisdom—the knowledge, understanding,
and instruction of God—is portrayed as
a woman! How cool is that! According to
Proverbs 1:20, she's shouting in the street
but few listen to or seek her. Do you?

Oh, the depth of the riches both of the wisdom and knowledge
of God! How unsearchable are His judgments and His ways
past finding out!
ROMANS 11:33 NKJV

No wisdom, no understanding, no counsel can avail
against the LORD.
PROVERBS 21:30 ESV

Wisdom [is] an understanding and application
of the moral principles of God.
JERRY BRIDGES

The fear of the LORD is the beginning of wisdom:
and the knowledge of the holy is understanding.
PROVERBS 9:10 KJV

How blessed is the man who finds wisdom and the man who
gains understanding. For her profit is better than the profit of
silver and her gain better than fine gold.
PROVERBS 3:13–14 NASB

A truly humble man is sensible of his natural distance from God. . .
of the insufficiency of his own power and wisdom. . .and that he needs
God's wisdom to lead and guide him, and His might to enable him to
do what he ought to do for Him.
JONATHAN EDWARDS

Don't be impressed with your own wisdom. Instead, fear the LORD
and turn away from evil.
PROVERBS 3:7 NLT

There is nothing more foolish than an act of wickedness;
there is no wisdom equal to that of obeying God.
ALBERT BARNES

Wisdom will protect you from the smooth talk of a sinful woman, who breaks her wedding vows and leaves the man she married when she was young.
PROVERBS 2:16–17 CEV

Where there is strife, there is pride, but wisdom is found in those who take advice.
PROVERBS 13:10 NIV

Listen to advice and accept instruction, that you may gain wisdom in the future.
PROVERBS 19:20 ESV

Wisdom is more precious than rubies, and nothing you desire can compare with her.
PROVERBS 8:11 NIV

Who is wise and understanding among you? Let them show it by their good life, by deeds done in the humility that comes from wisdom.
JAMES 3:13 NIV

But the wisdom from above is first of all pure. It is also peace loving, gentle at all times, and willing to yield to others. It is full of mercy and good deeds. It shows no favoritism and is always sincere.
JAMES 3:17 NLT

69

Work

God wants us to work hard at everything we set our hands to. After all, our work brings Him glory. So we women, who typically have less leisure time than men, should be good to go. Just be sure to balance your workload with the people in your life, as well as follow God's example by taking off at least one day per week.

The LORD God took the man and put him in the Garden of Eden to work it and take care of it.
GENESIS 2:15 NIV

"You have six days each week for your ordinary work, but the seventh day is a Sabbath day of rest dedicated to the LORD your God. On that day no one in your household may do any work."
EXODUS 20:9–10 NLT

Then Jesus said, "Let's go off by ourselves to a quiet place and rest awhile." He said this because there were so many people coming and going that Jesus and his apostles didn't even have time to eat.
MARK 6:31 NLT

You will again obey the LORD and follow all his commands I am giving you today. Then the LORD your God will make you most prosperous in all the work of your hands and in the fruit of your womb, the young of your livestock and the crops of your land.
DEUTERONOMY 30:8–9 NIV

Far and away the best prize that life has to offer is the chance to work hard at work worth doing.
THEODORE ROOSEVELT

I was one of those people who put too much emphasis on work and career and material possessions, and it took its toll on all my relationships, on my physical health, my emotional and mental health.
TONY SHALHOUB

If you plan and work hard, you will have plenty; if you get in a hurry, you will end up poor.
PROVERBS 21:5 CEV

"But as for you, be strong and do not give up,
for your work will be rewarded."
2 Chronicles 15:7 niv

We are merely moving shadows, and all our busy rushing ends in
nothing. We heap up wealth, not knowing who will spend it.
And so, Lord, where do I put my hope? My only hope is in you.
Psalm 39:6–7 nlt

We work to become, not to acquire.
Elbert Hubbard

The Lord helps the fallen and lifts those bent beneath their loads.
Psalm 145:14 nlt

He who tills his land will have plenty of food, but he who follows
empty pursuits will have poverty in plenty.
Proverbs 28:19 nasb

Nothing will work unless you do.
Maya Angelou

If anyone is not willing to work, then he is not to eat, either. For
we hear that some among you are leading an undisciplined life,
doing no work at all, but acting like busybodies.
2 Thessalonians 3:10–11 nasb

Who can find a virtuous and capable wife? . . .
She is energetic and strong, a hard worker.
Proverbs 31:10, 17 nlt

" 'Be strong, all you people of the land,' declares the LORD, 'and work. For I am with you,' declares the LORD Almighty."
HAGGAI 2:4 NIV

Work with enthusiasm, as though you were working for the Lord rather than for people. Remember that the Lord will reward each one of us for the good we do, whether we are slaves or free.
EPHESIANS 6:7–8 NLT

Work is not man's punishment. It is his reward and his strength and his pleasure.
GEORGE SAND

"Why work for something that doesn't really satisfy you? Listen closely to me, and you will eat what is good; your soul will enjoy the rich food that satisfies. Come to me and listen; listen to me so you may live."
ISAIAH 55:2–3 NCV

Find a job you like and you add five days to every week.
H. JACKSON BROWN JR.

Make it your ambition to lead a quiet life: You should mind your own business and work with your hands, just as we told you, so that your daily life may win the respect of outsiders and so that you will not be dependent on anybody.
1 THESSALONIANS 4:11–12 NIV

70

Worry

Women are born worriers. But 40 percent of
the things we worry about will never happen.
Ladies, that's a big leak of our energy. Instead
of wringing our hands over what might
happen, let's take our worries to God and
leave them there. Whew! That's a load off!

Cast all your anxiety on him because he cares for you.
1 PETER 5:7 NIV

Don't fret or worry. Instead of worrying, pray. Let petitions and praises shape your worries into prayers, letting God know your concerns. Before you know it, a sense of God's wholeness, everything coming together for good, will come and settle you down. It's wonderful what happens when Christ displaces worry at the center of your life.
PHILIPPIANS 4:6–7 MSG

"Therefore I tell you, do not worry about your life, what you will eat or drink; or about your body, what you will wear. Is not life more important than food, and the body more than clothes?"
MATTHEW 6:25 NIV

God never built a Christian strong enough to carry today's duties and tomorrow's anxieties piled on top of them.
THEODORE LEDYARD CUYLER

"And who of you by being worried can add a single hour to his life?"
MATTHEW 6:27 NASB

"Do not be anxious, saying, 'What shall we eat?' or 'What shall we drink?' or 'What shall we wear?' "
MATTHEW 6:31 ESV

*Worry does not empty tomorrow of its sorrow.
It empties today of its strength.*
CORRIE TEN BOOM

"Do not worry about tomorrow, for tomorrow will worry about itself. Each day has enough trouble of its own."
MATTHEW 6:34 NIV

*The strong hands of God twisted the crown of thorns
into a crown of glory; and in such hands we are safe.*
CHARLES WILLIAMS

"You will stand trial before governors and kings because you are my followers. But this will be your opportunity to tell the rulers and other unbelievers about me. When you are arrested, don't worry about how to respond or what to say. God will give you the right words at the right time. For it is not you who will be speaking—it will be the Spirit of your Father speaking through you."
MATTHEW 10:18–20 NLT

*Every evening I turn my worries over to God.
He's going to be up all night anyway.*
MARY C. CROWLEY

When my anxious thoughts multiply within me,
Your consolations delight my soul.
PSALM 94:19 NASB

Search me, God, and know my heart;
test me and know my anxious thoughts.
PSALM 139:23 NIV

Anxiety in the heart of man causes depression,
but a good word makes it glad.
PROVERBS 12:25 NKJV